LOST PLAYS
OF
SHAKESPEARE'S AGE

LONDON
Cambridge University Press
FETTER LANE

NEW YORK · TORONTO
BOMBAY · CALCUTTA · MADRAS
Macmillan

TOKYO
Maruzen Company Ltd

LOST PLAYS
OF
SHAKESPEARE'S AGE

BY

C. J. SISSON

*Lord Northcliffe Professor of
Modern English Literature in the University of
London*

CAMBRIDGE
AT THE UNIVERSITY PRESS
1936

PRINTED IN GREAT BRITAIN

CONTENTS

CONTENTS

PLATES

PREFACE

My object in this book has been as much to tell stories of life and people in Shakespeare's day as to add to our knowledge of the Elizabethan stage and drama or to record texts rescued from their burial in legal evidences and now submitted to the unforeseen test of literary criticism, which they can scarcely abide with equanimity.

I have therefore avoided footnotes as far as possible, and have relegated to an appendix a list of documents which have furnished me with material and are available for re-examination. I have also refrained from the exact reproduction of quotations and have generally extended abbreviations, except in so far as the texts themselves are recorded as literary documents, and also in documents of especial importance. I have even, on occasion, taken upon me to put narrative in dialogue form, while preserving the actual words of the document. I have not, however, modernised my sources. Those who may care to follow my steps through a jungle of law-records and other material will find, I hope, essential faithfulness in the use I have made of them for my purpose. The manuscript of the jig *Fool's Fortune*, for example, was as reverently examined and deciphered as if it had been a jewel of price, as indeed in its way it is. Mr A. E. Stamp, Deputy Keeper of Public Records, kindly checked with me some doubtful readings.

To Mrs J. E. Neale I owe the communication of the document containing the text of *Michael and Frances*, during my search for it. Mr Godfrey Davies of the Huntington Library kindly made a précis for me of the relevant Ellesmere manuscript, formerly at Bridgewater House. The Rev. J. O. Hichens, Vicar of Guilsborough, though aware of the trend of my story, magnanimously allowed me to consult his Parish

Registers to pursue my enquiries into the chequered career of his predecessor Nicholas Cartmell, who kept those Registers so well and loved his church, and thereby perhaps balanced his account in a more august Register. My colleague Miss Winifred Husbands has ensured accuracy, as far as is humanly possible, in the proof-reading, and has also kindly contributed the Index. And to the Bibliographical Society and the editors of *The Library* I am grateful for permission to reprint in a revised form the story of *Keep the Widow Waking*. The Society of Antiquaries has kindly permitted me to reproduce here part of the broadside relating to the murder plot of *Keep the Widow Waking*. My friend Professor Hyder Rollins allowed me to consult him upon the tunes to which reference is made. I had intended to give an account, in Chapter IV, of a May Game at Horncastle in 1601, but in the meantime this has been described in Mr N. J. O'Conor's *Godes Peace and the Queenes*.

I hope that this book may impart something of the pleasure that has lightened the path of exploration and that comes chiefly from intimate contact with Shakespeare's contemporaries, even if that intimacy is not invariably edifying.

C. J. SISSON

UNIVERSITY COLLEGE,
LONDON

June 1935

LOST PLAYS

OF

SHAKESPEARE'S AGE

Chapter I

INTRODUCTORY

It would be well enough if we could indeed know what song the sirens sung. It would perhaps be better still if we could know more about the scores of Elizabethan plays of which nothing remains but the bare mention of them in Henslowe's *Diary*. Titles survive, the names of authors, and even perhaps the sum of Henslowe's share of the takings day by day. But the flesh and blood of many a great play has been buried beyond recovery, and Henslowe only serves to make us the more sadly aware of the outrages that time and chance have wrought.

Ben Jonson told Drummond 'that the half of his comedies were not in print', and Henslowe's *Diary* bears witness to a number of lost plays in which he had a hand. What would we not give to have Ben Jonson's handling of a murder melodrama in *Page of Plymouth*? What light would be thrown on the art of Shakespeare in one of his greatest and most difficult plays, had Chettle and Dekker's *Troilus and Cressida* survived? How much of the full stature of Dekker, Chapman and Heywood has been hidden from us by the loss of so many plays written in the days of their strength? What obscure dramatists might possibly have stood forth revealed as not unworthy compeers with the great ones?

I am not ready to accept with confidence the belief that all the best of this abundant drama survived, and that the worst only is buried in the oblivion that fell upon almost all plays neglected by the printer. Nor am I without fear that we have lost a play of Shakespeare himself, in the *Love's Labour's Won* mentioned by Meres in 1598, which is so universally assumed, without cause, to be an alternative title to some one of the extant plays. We have no manner of certainty concerning the time when Shakespeare set up as dramatist. The accepted date, 1592, when the poet was already twenty-eight years of age, stands on a shaky foundation. And it may well be that several early plays from his hand went no further than the stage and never came into the hands either of printers in his lifetime or of his later colleagues in the Chamberlain-King's Company who collected his works in 1623. Certainly *Love's Labour's Lost* is the work of no prentice beginner, but of one expert already in high comedy.

Our sense of loss may well be heightened when we find evidence from other sources, hitherto unexamined, concerning Elizabethan plays of which no trace remains elsewhere, and when we find that these involve the work of some of the greatest dramatists of the period. Such evidence is to be found in the records of proceedings at law in the Court of Star Chamber. It may well be that the number may be increased as these and other contemporary manuscript records undergo more exhaustive search. From these records we derive not only information concerning the London stage and drama of the great age, but also light upon some minor forms of drama which the printed book ignores, for good reason.

We have long moved in the dark, for example, when discussing the Jig, which was so prominent a feature of the London stage as an afterpiece. What we know about the Jig can hardly be squared with such an example as we find appended to *Twelfth Night*. But in the records of Star Chamber we find at least two complete provincial specimens, with their text and with a full explanation of their origin and mode of performance. So with the provincial drama in general, and in particular with the obscure problem of those May Games which come so frequently under administrative notice, and whose nature is so little known.

To anyone familiar with the conditions of Elizabethan life

it might seem inevitable that the drama would furnish material for proceedings in Star Chamber as well as in the Privy Council. Topical foundations for a play, or topical references in a play, might affect either public or private susceptibilities, and lead to serious trouble.

Elizabethan and Stuart dramatists fell foul of royal authority often enough, as is well known. While it was tempting to cater for the topical interests of the audiences, and to profit thereby, it was a risky game. Ben Jonson was in trouble in 1597, along with Nashe, over *The Isle of Dogs*, and was imprisoned in the Marshalsea. He came before the Council again to answer for the political and religious implications of *Sejanus*, and in 1605 was imprisoned a second time, with Chapman, for his share in *Eastward Ho!* The satire upon the Scots, and the Scots King of England, would undoubtedly please the audiences of London. There is further evidence of this in Day's *Isle of Gulls* in 1606, as a result of which 'sundry were committed to Bridewell'. Even classical tragedy, in the shape of Daniel's *Philotas* in 1604, which is apt to weary a modern reader, created stir and excitement in its own day. For it was held by the Privy Council to be a reflection of the dangerous matter of the dead Earl of Essex. Four years earlier, indeed, Essex had foreseen such things in a complaint to the Queen:

Shortly they will play me in what forms they list upon the stage.

In 1599 Sir Francis Vere and Sir Robert Sydney were closely personated in a play upon the siege of Turnholt. Two years later the Curtain was presenting, less openly, but recognizably, other living persons of importance. And a contemporary letter of 1604 describes a play, upon the Gowry Plot, which went to the extreme length of bringing the King himself into dramatic action. This crowning indiscretion was laid to the door of the King's Men, and we may have some doubts about the matter. But there was no doubt that the French Ambassador took the strongest exception to the performance in 1608, by the Blackfriars Children, of Chapman's play *The Conspiracy of Biron*, with its portrait of the living King of France in a story of recent French history.

These plays, and others, were judged to be of seditious import, and to implicate the Crown or Crown policy. They were therefore dealt with by the Privy Council. Such were the perils of which Tilney, Master of the Revels and Censor of Plays, acting for the Lord Chamberlain, a Crown official, warned the authors and actors of the proposed play *Sir Thomas More*, when he sent it back to them with his orders for drastic revision. It was for this reason also that in 1631 Massinger had to set to work to transmute the Portuguese Don Sebastian and the Catholic Hermit of his *Believe as You List*, based on comparatively recent events, into the Syrian King Antiochus and the Stoic Philosopher of a sufficiently remote and fictitious antiquity.

Nor was it in London alone that such misdemeanours or indiscretions roused the attention of jealous authority. The records of Star Chamber furnish us with an infinity of details upon the strange and tragic story of a performance in Yorkshire, by a travelling company of provincial actors, of a play which set forth the life of St Christopher, in 1609. What might at first sight appear to be a harmless diversion of a country knight and his retainers takes its place, when the story is fully told, in dark and dangerous annals of strife, suspicion and conspiracy. For players and audience alike were Catholics. Their play ridiculed the Church by law established in England, and spread disaffection among its hearers. In all its circumstances and setting it was too closely related to the recent Gunpowder Plot to be lightly treated. It was nothing to the great ones of the Court and at Westminster Hall that the magic name of Shakespeare is evoked by these humble players, who included among their repertoire two plays fresh from the press, and toured all Yorkshire with the precious quartos of *King Lear* and *Pericles* which served them for prompt copies. The name which appeared upon both title-pages had but little significance to attentions riveted upon the names of hunted priests, Father Gerrard or Father Mushe, or of traitors dead in torment, Robert and Thomas Winter. The complexity of the issues involved in these events, however, and the wide ramifications of significant material bearing upon them, forbid inclusion of an account of this play in the present volume. It demands independent, and fuller, treatment.

But the stage could also cause offence to humbler antagonists, in its capacity as a mirror of events and persons of topical notoriety. And we find ourselves taken, in pursuit of such matters, into two of the principal London theatres, Paul's and the Red Bull, on the track of unrecorded plays of the highest interest, for one of them was the work of Chapman, and the other the joint work of Dekker, Webster, Ford and Rowley. We arrive at high circles when we examine the two sets of documents among the records of Star Chamber which report suits wherein citizens of London seek redress against actors and dramatists for stage comments upon their life and private affairs. I am bound to say that before reaching those great names we find ourselves moving in very low circles indeed, in that underworld of London which was apt to be so closely associated with the stage and the drama.

Both these plays contained material for accusations of libel and defamation, though neither was fought specifically or mainly upon this issue. The Court of Star Chamber had a long arm and a wide scope. In essence a judicial committee of the Privy Council delegated by the Crown, it investigated misdemeanours such as could not be satisfactorily dealt with in the ordinary process of law. It still maintained in theory its original status, as we may see from the occasional presence, under James I, of the King himself. During the greater part of its history it was a most valuable Court of Equity. Among other matters it enquired into conspiracies, libels, and interferences with justice. All three offences were capable of the widest interpretation, and injured parties could make it their business to discover and allege such implications in the making of plays for the popular stage to which they objected on personal grounds. If they were fortunate enough to persuade the Attorney-General that their complaint was of public importance, they had enlisted a valuable ally against a stage which had powerful interests behind it. It was the Attorney-General who, in the traditional formula, 'informed' the King that offences had been committed when the five London dramatists fell foul of their victims. In most cases, however, personal complaint was made when individuals felt themselves aggrieved on such grounds.

Among the many misdemeanours which came under the jurisdiction of Star Chamber, the offence of libel was the one which most enlivens its records, and it furnishes the searcher with a notable quantity of literary material of a sort. Libel found an inadequate place in the provisions of the Common Law. Nor could the Courts of Chancery or of Requests or of Exchequer deal with it, being concerned with property. But the Court of Star Chamber took a wider view of offences against the social order. And libel could take away what to many minds, especially in Elizabethan days, was of greater value than property even. The thought of the 'golden opinions' he has gained turns Macbeth against his dreadful crime, even though a crown was to be its reward, and in the end the loss of honour weighs heavily upon him. 'I have offended reputation', cries Antony in extremest bitterness of spirit. So with Cassio, whose lost reputation is 'the immortal part of myself'. It is in the mouth of Iago, of all men, that we find Shakespeare's most direct discourse upon the theme:

> Good name in man or woman, dear my lord,
> Is the immediate jewel of their souls:
> Who steals my purse steals trash; 'tis something, nothing;
> 'Twas mine, 'tis his, and has been slave to thousands;
> But he that filches from me my good name
> Robs me of that which not enriches him,
> And makes me poor indeed.

Elizabethan tragedy has no more frequent theme. It is the explanation of the uncompromising Elizabethan view of physical chastity, and justifies the suicide of Lucrece. Iago is but repeating the thoughts of Lucrece, who 'hath lost a dearer thing than life', leaving 'Lust, the thief, far poorer than before':

> Let my good name, that senseless reputation,
> For Collatine's dear love be kept unspotted:
> If that be made a theme for disputation,
> The branches of another root are rotted,
> And undeserv'd reproach to him allotted.

It is no small matter that Shakespeare shows us Othello transcending this powerful motive in his accusation of Desdemona. He could bear affliction, he tells her, and could have found patience:

> but, alas, to make me
> The fixed figure for the time of scorn
> To point his slow and moving finger at.

'Yet could I bear that too', he continues. Few Elizabethans could even have conceived that any motive could lie deeper than this, even the love of man for woman that Othello sees as the very spring of life for him. Heywood too shows love overtopping the thought of dishonour in *A Woman Killed with Kindness*, but it is a paradox which is illuminated by Anne Frankford's own comment:

> He cannot be so base as to forgive me,
> Nor I so shameless to accept his pardon.

Nothing less than her death can expiate his dishonour.

The intimate records of the lives of Elizabethans tell a thousand stories of men 'jealous in honour, sudden and quick in quarrel', either seeking or more often guarding 'the bubble reputation'. It was an age of litigation. And both Elizabeth and James frowned upon duelling:

> Cheveril cries out my verses libels are,
> And threatens the Star Chamber and the Bar.

When an Elizabethan, wounded in his reputation, seeks redress in Star Chamber, his Bill of Information sets forth in
its preamble how he has hitherto lived in good repute and
high esteem among his neighbours. This is the intangible
but precious possession which has been damaged. Richard
Harris, for example, a Colchester cleric, accused and libelled
by Brownist opponents in 1603, protests how he

ever Lived in good fame and reputation as well for his life and
conversation as for matters of doctryne.

Pecuniary damages, the mainspring of most libel actions of
today, are no ordinary part of an Elizabethan suit of the kind
with which we are concerned. The fines levied, in fact, fell
as welcome manna into the Royal Treasury.

The Bill of Information, fortunately, was compelled to
cite the actual libel wherever possible, either quoted within
the Bill or attached as a schedule to it. This method of procedure has preserved for us many a libel, in prose, in verse,
and not infrequently in dramatic form, often of high interest, though rarely of much literary quality. Unfortunately, the fates that preside over public records of earlier days,
preserving or destroying, or merely mislaying, have been
as capricious as Browning's Setebos. Among the many libels
that have survived, most are of merely curious interest, whatever their legal value. All throw light upon the real lives of
men and women, and help to fill in the picture of the background of Elizabethan life against which we see Shakespeare's
plays and other literature of honourable standing.

Had the fates been kinder, we might have found among
the wrack of these ancient controversies two complete
Elizabethan plays by authors of the first rank, both of them
Star Chamber matters. Chapman's play certainly appears to
have been an exhibit in the case in which he was a defendant.
If these plays have been irrecoverably lost, however,
we can at least reconstruct them in the main from the
abundant evidence given, and add to our knowledge

both of the Elizabethan drama and of the lives of these dramatists.

Thus, if this great prize has been lost, lesser prizes have been won. The libels preserved furnish numerous instances of the vogue of verse-satire throughout the country which never came into print and which illuminate the official history of printed literature. And when libel takes dramatic form in the provinces, as it frequently does, we find indispensable information, based on full and clear evidence, with complete texts, concerning such obscure types of drama as the Jig and the May Game in Shakespeare's age.

It is clear, indeed, that of the various ways of publishing a libel, none was so effective as presentation in dramatic form, and none was more congenial to the Elizabethan mind. It was laborious to spread a libel by written copies. It could, of course, be printed. But licences and facilities were not always easy to come by. And the printed word was on record, indisputable evidence, and dangerous. There was also more satisfaction in repeating or singing a libellous song in the streets or in taverns. There was an audience to share in the unseemly mirth, and it was a convivial proceeding. But a play or an interlude gave far fuller satisfaction, with its greater publicity and its conformity with an ancient and widespread love of dramatic spectacle, in which ribaldry played no small part. If this took the form in London theatres of full-blown professional plays, in the provinces a more elementary art was content with the Jig as its dramatic vehicle in the hands of amateur actors. There is no mistaking the pride of these provincials in their own labours in this field. So it is that the records of Star Chamber suffice to fill notable gaps in Elizabethan dramatic literature, in which hitherto no actual specimens have been available for study. Those now recovered, when inspected, make it understandable that none has come down to us in print. And the official dislike of the Jig on the London stage is fully explained and justified. It would seem clear that the London stage, like the provincial stage, was used to disseminate defamatory mirth, dispensing with the licence of the Master of the Revels for this part of its entertainments.

Action for defamation, in its many forms, was linked up wherever possible with an accusation of conspiracy, in order to bring it more definitely within the ambit of the Court of Star Chamber. So if a libel could be construed as part of a concerted plot to pursue illegal ends, the case was strengthened. And such an accusation is invariably made. The libeller is seeking to traverse a good marriage or to further an improper marriage. He is fomenting a breach of the peace. He is seeking to prejudice a Court of Law. He is offending against the ecclesiastical settlement of the country. He may be guilty of *Scandalum Magnatum*, bringing the Crown into disrepute through its nobles or its ministers. Or he may, in company with others, use a libellous publication as a move in what amounts to a treasonable conspiracy, as in the case of the Yorkshire Catholics and their play of *St Christopher*.

Considerable publicity attended the proceedings of Star Chamber at its meetings on Mondays and Wednesdays during the Law Terms. I have suggested elsewhere [1] that there is a curious parallel to be traced between Shakespeare's play of *As You Like It* and the quarrels of Thomas Lodge with his brother William which they ventilated in that Court in 1593. In a Nottingham case of 1617 it was suggested that if the libel in question came before Star Chamber it would give rise to a play in London. And in 1596 the Lord Treasurer himself, commenting upon a case, is reported as saying that he 'would have those that make the playes to make a Comedie hereof, and to act it with those names'. We cannot well help conceiving the possibility that the Star Chamber may have purveyed to the London stage a great deal of topical material, and that from its records much light may yet be thrown upon Elizabethan comedy. With such reason-

[1] *Thomas Lodge and Other Elizabethans* (Harvard University Press, 1933).

ings and instances we might perhaps associate the order from the Privy Council to the Middlesex Justices to suppress a libellous play which was being acted at the Curtain in May 1601.

It is grievous to think of the major documents of the un-known drama of Shakespeare's time that might have emerged in the course of search among Star Chamber re-cords, but have now vanished along with the numerous plays of the great age, the existence of which is known to us from various sources. But what has survived is of no mean value and interest. And in the setting of events and characters out of which these libels arose, they bring with them material for the never-ending drama of human life, and allow us to peer more closely into the intimacies of Elizabethan England. Courts of Law rarely exhibit human nature at its best. In them, and not least in these stories, we see the indelible stains of vice, cupidity, envy, jealousy, cruelty, hatred, that mar inexorably the face of man.

This was the England in which Shakespeare lived, the England which Shakespeare knew. But it was also the England of which Shakespeare was a part. In his nobler way he too was a faithful chronicler of his age, for the triumphs of human nature over human weakness, so resolutely set forth in his plays, are achieved in the face of a full measure of the evil overcome. The idyllic and heroic Elizabethan England of romantic fancy is no fit setting for Shakespeare's greatest plays.

Chapter II

PLAYS FROM THE LONDON STAGE

(i) *The Old Joiner of Aldgate*
by Chapman

§i. A LOST PLAY

George Chapman was already known in 1598 as a master of
both comedy and tragedy, as well as a poet who could
darken counsel in verse which made its exclusive appeal to
the intellectuals of his time. He had, in that year, gained
fresh laurels, this time in general estimation, by that
famous translation of Homer which, two hundred years
after, was to reveal a new world of poetry to Keats. And
he had shown his versatility, and his devotion to a young
dead poet who had moved in his own circle of friends,
in his completion of Marlowe's unfinished *Hero and Leander*,
also printed in 1598. But if Chapman's poetry has been preserved in print, most of those early plays which won him
renown have disappeared.

Henslowe records five plays of his in the years 1598–9 of
which none has survived, unless *The World runs on Wheels*
is a first version of *All Fools*. The loss is disastrous, and it is
felt more deeply in days when the greatness of Chapman
is becoming more fully realized. There is therefore an especial
interest in whatever can furnish some measure of compensa-
tion for the vanished 'tragedy of Bengemens plotte' that
Chapman wrote for Henslowe upon a scenario prepared by
Ben Jonson, or the pastoral tragedy of 1599 that would have
shown us a Chapman engaged upon pure poetry in

dramatic form, innocent of Stoic philosophy, an unknown Chapman indeed.

Failing this Chapman of infinite possibilities, another Chapman may at any rate now be revealed in some detail, a dramatist scenting out the makings of a play in certain odd proceedings in Newgate in his own time, writing the play as a private venture and selling it in the best market, baking and vending hot cakes of undoubtedly topical dough.

In February 1603 there was acted at the St Paul's house a play by Chapman, under the title of *The Old Joiner of Aldgate*. The play itself has not been preserved. But the record of it remains in legal documents, and it may be reconstructed with reasonable fullness, in the light of the information available in the records of Star Chamber and elsewhere upon the play and upon the complex and entertaining series of events in which it has its setting and which, indeed, it mirrors.

What we are able to learn should be of no small interest to the lover of Elizabethan drama. There is, in the first place, a story here, good enough for a full-dress novel, one that brings us into the closest intimacies of life in Elizabethan London and gives us in full detail the raw material out of which drama not only might arise but actually did arise. It is therefore a parallel and pendant to the story of *Keep the Widow Waking*, which occupies a later chapter here. In particular, a great deal of light is thrown upon the marriage-law of Elizabethan England and upon the significance of betrothal, a matter of importance for the understanding of Shakespeare's *Measure for Measure* and of the poet's own relations to Anne Hathaway.

Secondly, we have here a striking example of the stage-play of libellous content, if not actually of libellous purpose, bringing its author and producer into question in the Court of Star Chamber. Thirdly, we find George Chapman, at the very height of his career, descending to dramatic journalism, the least likely of men, we might have thought, to engage his genius in such a lowly task. For no dramatist, not even Ben

Jonson, shows a higher respect for his art than Chapman. Any future biographer of Chapman must needs be deeply concerned with the whole story.

Again, the story of this play must be taken into account when we consider the general problem of topical references in the Elizabethan drama, in which Shakespeare also has been involved, notably in recent years. Finally, there is some definite information upon the origin and history of an Elizabethan play and the procedure of its author and its producer. Persons of great interest in stage-history appear in the story and give evidence along with Chapman himself in Star Chamber.

For the laborious literary detective the task of reporting upon this strange episode of dramatic history has high interest. The threads of the story lead in many directions. Beginning from the thick and bulky dossier of the case preserved in the records of Star Chamber from the first year of James I, it leads both backwards and forwards in time to the records of the Court of Chancery, forwards to those of the Court of Requests, and backwards to those of the Delegates Court concerning matrimonial causes. As usual in such searches, their ramifications are as endless as those of life, and history, like the drama, must call an arbitrary halt. In reporting the result, a good deal of even relevant information must be excluded. A report must not develop into an Elizabethan Encyclopaedia.

§ ii. THE CITY HEIRESS AND HER SUITORS

The story has a heroine, I am glad to say. The question whether it has a hero or not must be decided after the story has been told. There are several candidates to choose from, but I doubt whether a scrupulous judge will care for any of them. In every properly conducted story, the heroine is bestowed in marriage upon the hero. But this is not a properly conducted story. It is real life. And it is Elizabethan life. And I cannot say that I am left with tender feelings towards the successful wooer of Agnes Howe. Agnes is of the right stuff for a heroine, if we may believe the unanimous evidence of a variety of witnesses, her friends and relations:

Agnes Howe hath byn of a softe & bashfull nature of modest & shamefast behaviour in the gouernement of her parents before her Aunte dyed & she hath euer synce for anything I euer hard to the contrary gouerned herself womanlye & is of good dyscression and behauiour & not childishe simple or sottishe.

If we could only add a further tribute to her, and assure ourselves that she was fair to look upon, we should have here a fairly typical *jeune première* of the Elizabethan drama. But there is an ominous silence on this question. All we hear definitely is that she was somewhat undersized. Her most persistent admirer, indeed, proposed deferring marriage with her for a year:

because she was then very young & of smale groweth.

Agnes was, in fact, seventeen years of age when this suitor thought her too young to be married yet. I do not think we should be justified in assuming that she was a beauty, even if in duodecimo. She had however, and this beyond all question, at least two thousand charms, if not three thousand, which dominate the tangled story of her wooing. For these are the various estimates of the fortune she inherited, valued in pounds sterling at these figures. We shall see, further, that Agnes develops less negative qualities as we proceed. Anthony Martin, who used to dine with Mrs Sharles, her wealthy aunt, every Sunday, testifies to Agnes' 'soft and tender nature', but ends with a 'but', at which point he was evidently cut off. Apparently he was going to be indiscreet. We shall hear her, for example, when offered claret wine by a suitor, speaking 'softly' yet quite decidedly to her mother, and demanding muscadine, a sweeter wine, also more potent, and nearly twice as expensive as claret.[1] We shall hear her

[1] John Eliot, *Ortho-epia Gallica*, 1593. Claret, red or white, 6*d*. a quart; Sack 8*d*. a quart; Muscadine and Malmsie, 10*d*. a quart.

breaking out into somewhat theatrical eloquence, and giving the most imperative judgments concerning the husband chosen for her. And finally we shall find her taking some of her affairs into her own hands, and somewhat conscious of her own importance as an heiress. She was, indeed, by high authority considered to be worthy of matching with an alderman's son, a noble destiny for a London girl of no pretensions by birth.

For Agnes was the daughter of a Barber-Surgeon, John Howe, who was evidently more Barber than Surgeon, and of no great distinction even in that profession. Indeed, we hear many uncomplimentary estimates both of his standing as a citizen and of his character. But Agnes had chosen her mother with more discretion. Not that Mrs Agnes Howe the mother was in herself an admirable character. She was not. But she had an affluent sister, Margaret Sharles, whose childlessness was looked upon with more than equanimity by the Howes. Agnes Howe and Margaret Sharles, I may add, were sisters of the printer George Harrison, and we shall find a number of Stationers entering into the story. Mrs Sharles, after the death of her husband William, a London Mercer, in 1590, was left with a considerable estate, including a fine house and shop called the Harrow in Christ Church, Newgate Market, and other lands and houses.

The history of the Harrow can be traced back to the third year of Edward VI, with the help of a Chancery suit of 1585. In 1549 the house was granted by the King, along with other lands and houses, to John Seymour, a relative of the Lord Protector. Seymour, of course, sold these properties, his agent being Nicholas Gower,

a short ffyne fellowe, and very wittye, and a good pen man.

Two lots were sold to Thomas Berthelet, the famous printer, then King's Printer, a house on Snow Hill and a garden in Turn Again Lane, both in St Sepulchre's, in July of the same year. At the same time William Witt bought the freehold of the Harrowe within Newgate from Seymour for £45. 13s. 4d. It was, as Witt said, 'but an old house of the olde fashone, and like not long to stande'. Witt was a saddler, and used the Harrow for both house and shop. John Judson, the printer, aged seventy-six on 10 December 1585, locates his own house for us by telling us that he lived opposite the Harrow. The association of the Harrow and its occupants with printers was thus of long duration. In December 1568 Witt sold the house to William Sharles for £120. It was rebuilt, all new from the ground up, whether by Witt or Sharles it is difficult to be sure. Judson says it was Sharles, after he bought it. The suit in Chancery arose on an allegation of defective title, which apparently Sharles was able to rebut. William and Margaret Sharles had evidently lived in the Harrow practically all their married life. Margaret was twenty-two years old in 1568, and thus was forty-four when her husband died in 1590.

The famous notary, George Kevall, of whom we shall hear again, drew up and witnessed William Sharles' will. Margaret continued to run the prosperous business, of which an important part was the sale of glass-ware, and it was certain that her heir would succeed to a pretty fortune. It was soon evident that she looked upon young Agnes Howe as her principal heiress, and before Mrs Sharles died Agnes was already an object of interest. There were rival claimants, however, and after the death of Mrs Sharles her will was questioned by Thomas Sharles, brother of her husband, on behalf of his daughters Suzan and Alice, and by Humfrey Wardner alias Barker, husband of her elder sister Christian. The will stood, however, after debate both in the Prerogative Court of Canterbury, and in Chancery.

We learn a good deal from these documents concerning the estate in question, especially from the will of Mrs Sharles, made on 2 September 1600. Mrs Sharles died on 11 September. She died at the age of fifty-four, confidently anticipating the joys of the Elect after the Day of Judgment, and in the meantime was buried beside her husband in Christ Church. Her will provides the usual legacies to her husband's Company, to numerous godchildren, the Vicar and the other poor of the parish, and to servants and old friends, the usual largesse of black gowns, and £20 to found a weekly preachership at Christ Church, in all not less than £400. She owned seven houses in the City and another at Clerkenwell, in addition to Barking Manor. The houses were bequeathed to various members of her family, but the principal house in Newgate, the shop and stock-in-trade, and all the residuary estate, were left in trust for her niece Agnes to John and Mrs Howe until Agnes should reach the age of twenty. Having provided further for a Herald at Arms to attend her funeral, Margaret set her mark to her will, being illiterate, and died nine days after.

Her estate, it seems, amounted to some two or three thousand pounds in value, and Margaret realized the dangers which lay in wait for so eligible an heiress as Agnes. She left instructions for Agnes that she was not to marry until she was twenty years of age, and that she was to be governed in all things, and especially with respect to marriage, by Margaret's very good friends the 'minister of Christ Church, Thomas Lyde, and by George Kevall',

desiring them ernestlie euen as my especial trust and confidence is in them to haue care of the good goverment (sic) of my said neece Agnes Howe and the bestowing of her in marriage.

Agnes was now seventeen. But if we are to believe the evidence, already three months before the death of Mrs Sharles she had been wooed by the earliest of the many suitors with whom the field was soon encumbered, and a fortnight before her death had actually been betrothed to him. And two months later, as a second suitor maintained, he had also achieved a contract of marriage with her. To understand these and other complications that ensued, it is necessary to turn our attention to a little-regarded but very active and interested figure in the background, to John Howe, the shadow behind the new throne of his richly endowed daughter.

Howe had been left a house in Warwick Lane and a black gown, out of all the wealth of his sister-in-law, as had his wife also. But they had been left to act as agents for Agnes until she reached the age of twenty. According to most accounts he was hard put to it to maintain himself by his own efforts. The question was bound to occur to him whether this was not an unreasonable state of affairs. And upon mature consideration he was bound to reflect further not only that it would be desirable to adjust the disproportion of Margaret's arrangements but also that he was placed in an unrivalled position of vantage for such remedial measures as he might conceive proper. The first step clearly was to obtain for himself administration of Margaret's will. The situation, with the Howes in full possession of the chief house and all Margaret's papers and goods, was impossible for Lyde and Kevall. Moreover, they made an attempt to obtain letters of administration, but failed, and therefore renounced in favour of Howe, on 2 December 1600. To regularize this, Howe had to deposit security for the value of the estate, in a bond of £2000.

The proceedings reflected no small discredit upon two of the Doctors of the Prerogative Court with whom the decision rested. The Star Chamber Bill is careful not to accuse the Doctors, but the evidence is too circumstantial not to be believed. Howe could not, in fact, back a bond for so great a sum, nor could he find adequate sureties. It is reported indeed that when Howe was reproved by his Company 'for detayning half a Crowne from some poore bodye', he was ordered to pay it back 'by sixe pence a weeke'; and Harrison the printer tells us that when Mrs Sharles died Howe had only a single gown, and had to get it out of pawn to do honour to the event. Mrs Sharles, moreover, had paid for the lease of his house.

Howe is shy of giving information about his own estate, and will only go so far as to say that five pounds would meet all his debts. But he put various points to the Doctors. There was, for instance, the natural hesitation of a man unused to high finance as to the best way of investing such large sums. Fortunately Dr Gibson, one of the Judges, had a suggestion to offer, during the preliminary discussions concerning the administration of the will. Dr Gibson was about a purchase and could use £300 or £400 out of Margaret's estate. It is Howe himself who tells the story. Howe refused to lend so much. But he lent him £150, expecting interest of course, even if it was not stipulated between such honourable men. And a further £150 was to follow, doubtless after the Court had come to the right decision. So Howe took a bond made out to himself. Howe shows surprise that Dr Gibson eventually refused interest, and insists that the transaction, though it heralded Gibson's grant of administration, had no bearing upon that grant.

Then, again, there was the problem of disposing honourably of such an heiress as Agnes, his daughter and ward. It is odd indeed that among the young men who sought to marry Agnes, however unsuccessfully, was a 'Doctor's son of the Arches'. Dr Gibson had a son and heir who entered with his father into the bond to Howe. It would seem that Howe had not appealed in vain to dignity and wisdom in this difficulty also. But it was Dr Dunne who proposed to Howe that Agnes should enter into his care, and arrangements were made to take Agnes into the country to Dunne's house on a Saturday and to marry her there next morning to one of his sons. Lyde put a stop to this scheme, as he tells us himself. And so Dunne refused administration to Lyde and Kevall, and Gibson granted it to Howe. The two Doctors were a pretty pair, and seem to have intended to share the spoils.

The problem of the disposal of Agnes was, in fact, Howe's chief preoccupation. But in the meantime there were other matters to attend to. There were, for example, many and great debts owing to Mrs Sharles, and now to the estate, which an energetic administrator might liquidate. Howe's notable mercy to the debtors aroused subsequent condemnation. To agree to a composition of six and eightpence in the pound for good debts savoured of improbable quixotism, and the real question was what financial byplay took place between Howe and the debtors. Again, with a chest full of bonds at his disposal, how easy it was to endorse some of them to himself. And as for money and plate, the process was still simpler. £200 in cash disappeared, for instance. So a great deal of feverish activity preceded Howe's submission of an inventory, and a notable diminution of Agnes' inheritance. Anthony Martin puts his depredations at £800, and offers to produce evidence. It is only fair to add that Howe explained the undoubted erosion of the assets, with a Falstaffian unconscionableness, by accusing the Rev. Thomas Lyde of embezzling goods to the value of £500, and of actually robbing the till of the shop, in the interval before administration was granted to Howe by the helpful Dr Gibson. Lyde admits, it is right to say, that Howe paid out £300 for the funeral of Mrs Sharles.

Having done what he could in these directions, Howe addressed himself to the major problems of Agnes and her marriage. Here he proceeded to involve himself in a series of negotiations of surprising complexity, through which runs only one clear thread to guide Howe, his desire to free this one maiden from the oppression of her own wealth, as far as might be, and to transfer the burden to himself. The suitors were many and eager. First in the field was John Flaskett, here described as a bookbinder in Paul's Churchyard, and worth not less than £60 in his estate, and possibly as much as £300. We hear a good deal of him in the records of the Stationers' Company. We may remember that George Harrison, Stationer, was one of the uncles of Agnes, and doubtless he had some hand in bringing Flaskett into touch with the Mercer's family. While this matter was in the end to bring Flaskett into Star Chamber, it was not his first experience of this Court. He had been brought into question there as a minor defendant, along with John Harrison and John Legatt, the Cambridge University printer, in a suit concerning the printing of Sidney's *Arcadia*, in November 1600. Ponsonby, to whom the copyright belonged, accused them of a conspiracy to pirate the *Arcadia*, by importing into England an Edinburgh edition printed to Harrison's order, and selling it in the English market. The matter was referred to the Stationers' Company, and Flaskett paid his fine of fifty shillings for his share on 2 April 1601.[1] A few months before, Flaskett together with Cuthbert Burby had interfered similarly with a copyright of William Aspley, 'touchinge the booke of the duche voiage into thindies 1588'.[2] And again in September 1602 he was involved with Burby, Jaggard and others in a complaint by Ling and others.[3]

The marriage of Flaskett with Agnes was first broached as early as in June 1600, apparently, some months before the death of Mrs Sharles. So John Oswald tells us. Oswald was also a Stationer and bookbinder, and was, in fact, Porter to the Stationers' Company since 1592.[4] If we believe some of the evidence, Oswald devil-portered it, and trod the dangerous primrose path of drunkenness and perjury, aggravated by poverty, a peculiarly Elizabethan misdemeanour. But here we may accept Oswald's history, for he had nothing much to gain by telling it. It was he who thought of securing the rich prize for a brother-Stationer:

Aboute June last was two yeres.... I did first knowe by the relacion & reporte of Agnes How mother of Agnes Howe vsed

---

[1] *Records of the Court of the Stationers' Company*, pp. 80–81; Star Chamber Proceedings, 5. P. 5/6; P. 65/10.
[2] *Records of the Court of the Stationers' Company*, p. 50.
[3] *Ib.* p. 91.
[4] *Ib.* p. 42. He is identifiable by signatures in the Stationers' Court Book and at the foot of his deposition in Star Chamber.

vnto my wife that Mrs Sharles...would make Agnes How the daughter worthe three Thowsand Pounds, And that I was the first that moved the matter of Marriage betwixte John fflaskett ...& Agnes Howe the daughter, I having vnderstanding by the reporte of Agnes Howe the mother that her daughter shoulde be lefte worthe so great a porcion & therevpon I in goodwill vnto...fflaskett moved him in the matter of marriage.

Flaskett tells us that it was actually Mrs Howe who suggested the idea to Oswald in the first place. At any rate he welcomed the suggestion and bade Oswald God-speed in his efforts to arrange the matter. Over a month before Mrs Sharles' death he had so far progressed that he had brought together in his house in Knightrider Street the mother, the daughter, and the suitor. He then proposed that Mrs Sharles should be approached by Mrs Howe and Flaskett, and Mrs Howe subsequently told him that Mrs Sharles approved. Here we are on less firm ground, and a still more doubtful statement follows, namely that Agnes

was contracted with...fflaskett...& that...Agnes &...fflaskett were contracted together in this defendants howse in the halle thereof in the moneth of August last was two yeres abouts fortnight or three weeks before the death of... Mris Sharles,

i.e. in August 1600. This statement, when it was made, was hotly debated. It was, however, fully supported by Oswald's wife Rose and by Flaskett himself, who gives details concerning the progressive stages of this short courtship. And further information comes from Mrs Howe and other witnesses. The first important step was taken when Flaskett walked abroad with Agnes, though not alone, of course. On a Sunday in July 1600, the Oswalds came to Mrs Howe's house. She was not feeling well, and they proposed an excursion to Lambeth. So forth they went, on their way to Trigg Lane Stairs to take boat across the river to St George's Fields and so to Lambeth. By a happy chance, as they went down Trigg Lane who should meet them but John Flaskett, who joined the party to Lambeth! And on the return journey, Mrs Howe, as she tells us,

> by the waye being not well Complayned therof and therevpon they went in together to [the Kings] a Taverne in olde ffishe streete (the signe she Certenly remembreth not)[1] and ther dranck some sacke, which she thincketh...fflaskett paid for.

Next morning, on the Monday, Flaskett was at Oswald's house, and felt some concern whether the sack had operated favourably. Therefore, still proceeding by *oratio obliqua*, he sent Oswald to enquire after Mrs Howe's health. The ambassador returned with a message that if Flaskett could await her, she would presently arrive in person, with her daughter. So Flaskett, as far as his knowledge went. But Oswald tells a better story, which must be given in full, of that morning's events: Mrs Howe, he said (I turn the narrative into the first person),

> coming in the morninge of that day abouts 8. of the clocke vnto my house then saied to me these words viz Yesterday we had good cheere at Lambeth with Mr fflaskett & I could eate nothinge I would I had some now, wherevnto I answered that Mr fflaskett was the same man as he was before and that I would fetch him to my house if she would fetch her daughter thither which she saied she presently would & then she departed from my house for her daughter, and presently after I repaired vnto fflaskett & acquainted him what Agnes the mother had saied to me & that she purposed to bring her daughter presently to my house, I then wishing fflaskett to come thither & to bestow something vpon them.
>
> And therevpon fflaskett gave me ii*s*. vi*d*. to buy & provide something for them to eate & therevpon I departing from fflaskett did buy a pinte of white wine & a pinte of clarett & bredd & butter & some other victualls & brought the same to my house, And Agnes Howe the mother & her daughter & fflaskett being com to my house & sitting downe at the table together & I in their companie to eate & drinke, Agnes the daughter whispered

---

[1] *The Kings* deleted. It was, in fact, the Boar's Head.

her mother in the eare & I then asking Agnes the mother what the matter was she aunswered that her daughter would drinke no white nor clarett wine but would have a pinte of Muskadine, & therevpon fflaskett willed me to fetche a pinte of Muskadine, which I did, and after these persons had dranke the wyne

the serious business before the meeting was dealt with. The white wine, it appears, was for Flaskett himself, who drank no claret. Agnes, who 'did speake softely to her mother' to that effect, drank neither, and so had her pint of expensive muscadine. And Mrs Howe and the two Oswalds, it would seem, shared one poor pint of claret between the three, a pennyworth each. So Oswald addressed Mrs Howe; and we may now give the matter in dialogue form:

Oswald (*to Mrs Howe*) Mris Howe we haue had often meetings together but no speches to know whether Mr fflaskett shall haue your daughter to wife   are you content that Mr fflaskett shall haue your daughter to wife.

Mrs Howe   yea with all my harte I like well of him.

Oswald (*to Agnes*)   how saiest thou Anne   art thou contented likewise.

Agnes   yea truly if my mother be so contented.

Oswald   then give Mr fflaskett thy hand & speake thy minde.

Agnes (*giving her hand to Flaskett*) I doe take you for my husband.

Flaskett (*holding Agnes' hand*) I doe take you for my wife. (*Kisses her. They drink to one another.*)

And so the two were formally betrothed, in the presence of witnesses, Mrs Howe and John and Rose Oswald.

No tokens were interchanged, but Flaskett subsequently sent two pairs of gloves to the ladies, and on the day after the betrothal Agnes came to Oswald's house and gave him 'a sweetballe to give from her vnto...fflaskett'. While Flaskett agreed to Mrs Howe's proposal that the marriage should be postponed for a year, nevertheless he considered himself to be Agnes' husband and frequented her company during the rest of the lifetime of Mrs Sharles. More than this, Flaskett arranged with the wife of Edward Wood, a Cornhill mercer, for Agnes to stay and live with her, at Flaskett's expense,

to see and learne fashions because she was but young for the space of a yere...vntill he should marry with her.

Mrs Howe had refused Flaskett's first proposal, that Agnes should have a finishing course at his uncle Wright's house, but she agreed to this. And it looked like business.[1] And soon after the death of Mrs Sharles Edward Wood, being at her house, was with Mrs Howe and Flaskett when she was busy opening a chest full of goods and bonds. Mrs Howe then spoke to Flaskett:

Here is goods enogh John here wilbe enogh for you I hope   I care not if you will lett me have the house as long as I live and when I die it shalbe yours.

Such is the story of Flaskett and the Oswalds. We shall return to it later. But it would seem that at this stage, before Agnes came into her fortune, and before John Howe had put his finger well into the pie, he was faced with a betrothed daughter. And he had been left out in the cold. The problem became more acute, obviously, on the death of Mrs Sharles, when Howe seems to have heard about Flaskett's wooing for the first time. It is alleged that he demanded and got a loan of fifty shillings, and a promise to make it up to £10, from Flaskett, in return for his sanction. But this was clearly only a nibble taken as opportunity offered. He seems to have agreed to the marriage in the meantime. Henry Trym was present one day after the death of Mrs Sharles, in company with father, mother and daughter, and Flaskett, and heard Howe and Mrs Howe agree then that Flaskett should have Agnes if he would allow them

to hold the same house during their lyves & to sell their glasses there as...Margaret Sharles was wont to doe before.

[1] Agnes was not to suffer the unhappy fate of Pamela's Prudiana, in Richardson: 'Poor, miserable Prudiana!...what a sad, sad fall was hers! And all owing to the want of a proper Education too.' (*Pamela*, Letter 134.)

But Howe had greater hopes in view. There were abortive negotiations with Dr Dunne and his son. And thereafter there was a spate of suitors with whom Howe negotiated one after another, if not indeed all at the same time. In this he had friendly help, and he needed it.

A little family group of conspirators, Mrs Howe tells us, could be seen 'often conferring and whispering together' on these various possibilities. Mrs Howe, when the matter came to enquiry, dissociated herself from such proceedings, but there is no doubt whatever that she had the most perfect opportunity for bearing witness to such plottings, and was in fact one of the group. The others were Peter Howe, John's brother, Agnes Shaw, Peter's daughter, and Joan Daniell alias Coppians, John's sister, all united by their family ties to bring as much money as possible into Howe pockets.

The two principal competitors with Flaskett for the favour of Howe were Thomas Field, a Hertfordshire gentleman with lands at Digswell, and Henry Jones, the son of a Welsh gentleman, John Jones, of the City of Gloucester, to whom, as one witness put it, Howe 'sold' Agnes and made bargains with them for her hand. Field was Peter Howe's candidate, so Mrs Howe tells us. He was welcomed at the Harrow on the day of the funeral of Mrs Sharles, and declared his intentions on the very day. After reasonable debate, definite proposals were formulated on 10 October 1600, when Field signed two bonds to Howe. First Field was bound in a thousand marks to ensure that within two days after his marriage with Agnes he would lease the Harrow to Howe for forty shillings a year for twenty-one years, the house being worth £40 a year. Second, he was bound in £500 to make over to Howe and Mrs Howe all the goods in the shop, including glass, wood-ware, wicker-ware and other stock. Evidently it was a miscellaneous business for a Mercer. The scrivener, Richard Wright, who drew up the bonds, gives these facts. Incidentally, he was a suitor himself, but he does not tell us what his own offer was.

Field's proposals satisfied Howe, at any rate. In the meantime Agnes' second betrothal had already taken place, in the afternoon of Friday, 3 October 1600, after dinner, that is to say, about a month or five weeks after her betrothal to Flaskett. On the Thursday before, Field sent word to the Howes at the Harrow that he would call upon them. He arrived in the morning, dined there with the family, and was kindly entertained and welcomed. After dinner Field and Agnes went together into a great chamber upstairs, with her mother, her aunt Joan Coppians, and her cousin Agnes, daughter of Peter Howe, and 'did sitt & talke familiarlie a great while'. A friend called to see Field, who went down, and soon returned. He now addressed Agnes, and here I turn again to dialogue:

Field (to Agnes) Now sweeteheart I should have gone awaie yesterdaie & was requested to stay, but now Mr Smith is come for me & I must take my leave of yow.... And now sweete heart I pray yow tell me your mind plainlie how you are affected towards me & whether yow can be content to forsake all men for my sake & to take me to your husband.

Agnes (rising from her seat & coming to Field at the foot of the bed) I am content to loue & lyke yow above all men & to take yow for my husband.

Field Your words sweete heart doe greatlie comfort my heart that you can do so. *(takes Agnes' hand, and holding it)* I protest before god sweete heart that I loue thee above all the women in the world & I take thee to my wife & therevpon I give thee my faith & trothe & if thou canst doe the like to me give me thy hand *(lets her hand fall)*.

Agnes (gives Field her hand) I can & I doe & therevpon I give yow my hand & my faith.

Field then kissed Agnes and gave her two pieces of gold 'in corroboration',

& then (they) kissed togither again, *which she thankfullie received*

as her cousin Agnes remarked enviously. And Joan Coppians pointed the moral:

Now god give yow ioy cosine for now yow are Mr ffeilds wife.

Such, at any rate, was the story of Joan Coppians and the cousin of Agnes, as well as of Field himself.

The ritual and the words, if used as thus reported, certainly made a ceremony binding in law. They approximate closely to those described in another case of precontract that has come to my notice, where there was very careful preparation, with the witnesses well tutored by two lawyers:

John Pigeon with his right hand takeinge Anne Louche by the right hand in loveinge and kinde manner saied, I doe here before God and this Company take thee to my wife and doe here promise never to marry any other but thee dureinge our life, And that I doe giue thee my faith and troth and soe loosed each others hands.

Thereupon Anne took his hand and repeated a similar form of words, and the ceremony was completed. An interesting parallel may be found in Lyly's *Mother Bombie*, Act IV, Sc.1. There remained only confirmation by the Church, and consummation. It appears to be a matter of importance that the witnesses were not servants or residents in the house of the parties. We may take this form for a model of the ceremony of contract of marriage. Its impugners in this case, at any rate, could only protest that it was too perfect to be true, and allege professional collusion and perjury. So here, if Field was only able to maintain his position when it came to producing evidence, his case was unassailable.

The third important candidate was Henry Jones. Negotiations took place between his father and Howe when father and son were staying in Howe's house in St Gregory's near Paul's. As far as I can see, they actually bid higher than any of their competitors. For the father entered into a statute of either £2000 or 2000 marks. But it was to ensure a jointure of £100 a year to Agnes. And this one-sided proposal did not appeal to Howe, who demanded more serious consideration for his own claims. Mr Jones made some offer to Howe. But my impression is that the Gloucester man thought he could manage without Howe, if it came to the push. An attempt indeed was made to carry Agnes off to Gloucester, but it failed. So Jones was left with a mere claim that Agnes had called him husband, and that he had called her wife, before witnesses, and that therefore there was a contract.

There were, to my knowledge, at least five other suitors, with all of whom Howe negotiated, either in rapid succession or indeed simultaneously. A certain Povey offered a jointure of £80 a year to Agnes, the house and wares to her parents, and in addition presented her mother with a hundred angels in return for the one he was to receive in marriage. Then there was a mysterious 'Humphrey of the Court', who had evidently descended from Whitehall circles into the City in search of wealth, and was prepared to stoop to conquer Agnes' fortune.

Chapman gives his full name as Humphrey Rogers, and there is no doubt that he was the Keeper of the Council Chamber so often referred to in the Acts of the Privy Council, whose year's budget advanced gradually from £10 in 1582 to £13. 6s. 8d. in 1588, and to £24 in 1598,

for his attendaunce and paynes taken and for provision of boughs, flowers and other necessaries for the Chamber, and for his chardges in the Progresse tyme for his stuffe and lodginge for one whole yeare.

Before Agnes' affairs were settled, Rogers had to make room for a Scottish partner, Alexander Douglas, in May 1603, to share his office with him. King James, no doubt, liked to see a familiar face in charge of the Chamber. It would seem that Rogers must have been a sadly mature suitor for Agnes, if he were indeed the 'Humphrey of the Court' in question. For he had held his office at Court since 1582 at least, when the girl was not yet born.

Wright the scrivener, Cox and Leer are known by name as suitors who dealt with Howe and joined in the unseemly auction with Humphrey and the rest. And there were others whose names even are not mentioned.

Unfortunately for Howe, these complications of Agnes' marriage affairs could not be conducted with complete secrecy. The three favourites, Flaskett, Jones and Field, got wind of each other's pretensions. Consequently, being true Elizabethans, they flew to the appropriate Courts of Law, in this case the Ecclesiastical Courts, each of the three in search of a declaration of a contract of marriage and of an injunction against the marriage of Agnes to any other person. Jones, who had the weakest case, was the first to appeal, and he went to the Consistory Court of London. Field followed suit in the Court of Arches, and finally Flaskett, also in the Court of Arches, on 11 February 1601. And so Agnes found herself defendant in three suits against three aspirants to her hand, all claiming to be contracted.

The question was clearly one that interested the little world of Howe's neighbours. It was bound to be spread all over London by Flaskett's printer friends, and by the general gossip of this most gossipy age and place. The lawyers would exchange amused notes upon it in the various Inns of Court. And, finally, Jones added a touch of genius to the debate. For he gave his grievance the fullest publicity in Agnes' own parish church, and

caused a Process to be executed and fixed vpon a Sonday or Holliday at & vpon the dore of the parish church of Christchurch London in the tyme of devine service & to stand there during the whole...service, att which tyme...Dr Milward was the ordinarie Preacher of the...Church.

We may imagine the citizen church-goers halted by such a notice, thronging round it, all agog to see how Mrs Howe and Agnes would take it, and all the dark hints, the broad jests, and secret confidences exchanged from knot to knot of onlookers. Truly, Dr Milward would need all his eloquence that morning to lead his congregation away from a good jest to pious thoughts. Was this a scene that Chapman could have used for a play?

So, in February 1601, a few months after the death of Mrs

Sharles, the situation had reached the full height of its complication, it would seem. Howe and Mrs Howe sat tight in Mrs Sharles' house and shop. Howe had embezzled a great deal of Agnes' estate. He had driven Lyde and Kevall out of the field. He had, moreover, guarded against surprise by the legal fiction of a deed of gift of what was left to a friend Thomas Pigott. He had bought for himself, at a cost of over £150, an office as a corn-measurer. And he had got himself deeply involved in devices to make his daughter's marriage further profitable to himself. Three of the suitors had got out of hand. Of these, Field was Howe's own especial candidate, Flaskett was Mrs Howe's nominee, and Jones ran a forlorn hope. The lawyers and the Ecclesiastical Courts, with which the game had started, had entered again and taken charge.

Surely we have completed what Ben Jonson would have called the protasis and the epistasis. The catastasis was due to intervene. Neither Ben Jonson nor Chapman could have imagined a more dramatic, a more unexpected turn to the story than that which in fact occurred. Chapman was acquainted with Howe, by sight at least. There can be little doubt that he was in closer touch than he would admit with several of the persons of the story, and that he followed the story with interest. And he could not fail to have seen its possibilities, even before the surprising turn of tide which must have been decisive to the dramatist in search of a comic theme.

§ iii. THE END OF THE STORY

The heiress Agnes Howe was now left in an unhappy plight, with a triple betrothal alleged against her, as defendant in three suits brought against her in the Ecclesiastical Courts by her three contracted suitors, Jones, Flaskett and Field—proceedings which her father was bound to look upon with some trepidation, especially in view of his maladministration of his daughter's estate. Contemplating this lamentable and embarrassing result of his negotiations, he looked around him for advice. He evidently considered that Flaskett had in fact a good case. But he was anxious that Field should prevail. He therefore sought an authoritative opinion concerning the validity of such a betrothal, and desired to know how Agnes might be freed from her alleged precontract with Flaskett. He had had experience of the expensiveness of advice from the Doctors of Ecclesiastical Law. And he was not on such terms with Lyde as would permit of approaching him. Lyde and Kevall were entirely opposed to all these suitors and were thinking in terms of aldermen's sons or other eligible young men of higher status than any of the bidders for Howe's consent and aid.

To whom should Howe turn? Fortunately, he thought, there is Lyde's colleague, Dr John Milward, the Preacher at Christ Church, a sober and judicious man of some thirty-five years of age, and a Doctor of Divinity. To him, therefore, Howe betook himself. I do not know what advice Dr Milward gave Howe. But I do know that the problem riveted the attention of the preacher, who gave it earnest consideration. Indeed, Dr Milward thought it well to take higher advice on the matter, and went himself to Dr Creake and Dr Hone in Doctors' Commons to ask whether a man might marry a woman who was then in suit concerning a former contract. I imagine that the answer was not entirely unsatisfactory.

For the next important event in this history was the immediate result of these negotiations, namely, the sudden marriage of Agnes to Dr Milward himself. This was executed with admirable celerity, at the parish church of Barnet in Hertfordshire, with the help of Milward's brother, the Rev. Mathias Milward, then Rector of the parish, and with no notion of obtaining Howe's consent. Howe must have reflected ruefully, on hearing the news, that in these bad latter days it was impossible to trust anybody. But there was a certain poetic justice in this solution of the problem, and in the hoisting of Howe by his own petard.

Dr Milward's wooing was short enough. It is clear that he succeeded in dazzling Mrs Howe with the prospect of such a marriage, and that in the two conferences which he had with her he won her over to his project. For Mrs Howe went to church to see her daughter married to Milward. It does not appear that he ever discussed the matter with Agnes herself in person. But he enlisted the sympathy of Mr and Mrs Lyde, and Mrs Lyde carried letters from Milward secretly to Agnes. Indeed, his proposal met with general approbation, except from Howe and from his rivals, and it seems evident that Agnes herself found both her taste and her ambition satisfied in Milward.

So far we have not considered this aspect of the matter. Yet it is worth considering. Indeed, Agnes begins to emerge as a much more complex character than appeared at first sight, when we gather evidence on this point. To begin with, Agnes had reserved judgment throughout all the preliminary negotiations with which Howe and Mrs Howe had busied themselves. She had, in fact, told her cousin Agnes Shaw, who was busy recommending Field to her, that

she would not marry with anye man in England till god had putt into her mynde whome she should marry which was all the answer that this defendant could gett of her in that behalf.

The close enquiry that was conducted in Star Chamber into Agnes' relations with her suitors reveals, in fact, a definite persecution of Agnes by her father to plague her into consenting to marry Field. Agnes Shaw, for example, was sent to haunt her to this intent, as we have seen. Howe himself admits that he agreed with Field that he should have Agnes, on the advantageous terms offered, and

thinking Field to be a very fitt match for his daughter, did in his fatherly Care perswade her to affecte him for marriage,

and so he arranged for Field to meet Agnes and to press his

suit himself. But his fatherly care took such strange shapes as might well furnish material for the pitiless comedy of which the Elizabethan stage was capable in its mood of satire. Agnes, in fact, did not like Field. Her mother admits that Agnes 'could never abide him nor indure his sight or presence'. She would indeed take refuge in her bedroom and lock herself up there. Whereupon Howe would many times command her to open the door and let Field in, or else he would come up and make her open it. But Mrs Lyde tells us that Agnes would defy even such a threat. Elizabeth Abbott, a servant in the house, tells us of worse things:

on a tyme because...Agnes in the hearing of...John Howe dyd miscalle...ffilde & envay in spiche against him shewing her dislike of him...John Howe dyd offer to have beaten her & had beaten her if Mris Lyed had not rescued her from him and all was bycause she miscalled...ffild & would not by any means consent to marry...ffilde.

Indeed there is ample evidence that the girl was made thoroughly miserable, and expressed her feelings in such lamentable and characteristic Elizabethan rhetoric as is quoted in an interrogatory and in certain depositions. Has she not, it is asked,

said verie often I will rather hange my selfe or kill my selfe then euer marrie ffeild...by reason of her fathers inforcement hath she not often wept & said I will dye at the doore & be torne in peeces with wild horses rather than euer marrie ffeild, for I cannot love him nor abide his company.

Such things indeed Agnes has said, 'with weeping teares', to Mrs Lyde, to Elizabeth Abbott, and to her mother, who all quote them with zest.

Then, finally, there was the mysterious episode of the pursuivants. One day, on 3 October 1600, when the Howes were at dinner at the Harrow, with Field and others as their guests, the following incidents occurred, fully related in an interrogatory put to Howe:

Did you...as you and...ffeilde your wyfe & daughter sitting

at dynner and Johan Daniell beeinge there and others, beginne to talke of Pursuivants that laye in wayte for your daughter & would take her awaye and soe she should be marryed to some vagrante fellowe, or such lyke and noe frend she had should have ioy of her and did not one of the mayd servants Retourne from the Ale house with beere, sent by you, in fearefull manner saye before you, or them that ther was twoe men att the sayd Alehouse that sayed they would pull the tyles of the house but they would pull your daughter out, and had warrante for her, and did not your wyfe then crye out alas that euer I was borne my daughter shalbe Carryed Awaye and did not you saye looke you daughter weare you not better marrye Mr ffeilde then be so vsed and did they not in that feare and affraightinge her shutt the wearhouse dore and did not your daughter Rune vpp into the house & hide her selfe and there after came vpp Joane Daniell your sister and Anne Shawe and did not you carrye vpp... ffeilde and cause the dore to be locked to them that they in that forme might enforce or procure her to be contracted   And...did not your daughter crie and weepe that night sayeinge   O mother my father hath made me take A peece of gould of ffeilde and I cannot love him,   And also the verye next daye...would not you have beaten your daughter because she would not yelde to Marrye ffeilde, but that she was Rescued from you.

The question goes on to quote Agnes' proposals for violent death in preference to such a marriage.

Other accounts add details and variant readings for an interested dramatist to choose from. Joan Daniell or Coppians, for example, came to the Harrow after dinner and was met by Mrs Howe in great distress:

Lord sister what a trouble have we with Nan   my maied went for drinke today & she brought worde that there were Pursivants about the house to take her away, I would to God we could perswade her to marry Mr ffeild for he is an honest gentleman,

to which Joan replied that Field was in fact an honest gentleman, but Nan 'may doe as she will'. The pursuivants, it seems, were actually in George Harrison's house near by. There were two of them, and they had a warrant in their pockets. Mrs Howe's version was perhaps the best for

Chapman's purpose. And it falls readily into dramatic form. Mrs Howe and Agnes are sitting quietly together. (The servant Elizabeth Abbott has been sent out for beer.) To them enters John Howe:

Howe   There were yesterday three or fower Pursivants at the doore and there are some to day to fetche and take awaye your daughter   And were you not better to lett ffilde marrye her then that she should be taken away by some beggarlye fellowe or Courtyer and so we shall have no ioye or comfort of her.

(*Enter Elizabeth Abbott, in alarm.*)

Elizabeth   Mris, Mris, there bee men at Mris Harrisons who swear they will pull the tiles of the howse but they will have Agnes Howe your daughter awaye with them.

Howe   looke you, were not you better to lett ffilde have her then she should be taken awaye in this sort.

Mrs Howe   Alas, alas, yet I had rather ffild should have her then she should be so caste away.

Both Mrs Howe and Agnes were 'putt into great feare Therby'.

This is excellent for drama. But Mrs Howe was perhaps a dramatist herself when she told the story thus, for she was then anxious to show that she was no party to her husband's schemes with respect to Field. Her report of Howe's words incidentally reveals her opinion of two of the suitors, the beggarly fellow being Jones and the Courtier being 'Humphrey of the Court'. It appears, in fact, that the pursuivants were employed by Henry Jones, as Howe quite credibly tells us. There was only one, in reality, who had a warrant to apprehend Howe, not Agnes, to make him enter into a bond not to allow Agnes to marry anyone but Jones. In the end he caught Howe, who was under arrest for a while upon this warrant. But in the meanwhile Howe used Jones' watchdog with great dexterity to terrify his daughter, if possible, into taking the quite irrevocable step of actual marriage with Jones' rival Field. He seems, indeed, to have brought her to some form of betrothal that afternoon. No dramatist could have conceived a more ingenious turning of the tables upon Jones. The complex intrigues of Elizabethan comedy were at least equalled in real life, as we may well observe here.

His intentions, according to his own report, were quite different. His sole object in sending Agnes upstairs to her room, whither Field subsequently followed her, was to ensure her safety from the pursuivant. It is true that after Agnes had contracted herself to Field, Howe

did sometymes by faire speches & sometymes by sharp speches perswade his...daughter not to breake her promise to him,

and after Agnes had uttered those absurd and irreverent remarks about wild horses and drowning and so forth Howe reproved her for such words. But he is very grieved at the suggestion that he had

moste vnnaturallye & vnkindlye euer sought by letters sutes of lawe guifts and all perswacions to drawe her from her husband to whom she ys marryed to the end she might accepte of... ffeilde or fflaskett with whome (he had) Compounded.

From this accusation it can be realized at once that when Agnes married Dr Milward the matter was by no means closed. Indeed, the real battle now began, with all the serious combatants in the field. Dr Milward and Agnes had, in fact, committed a grave indiscretion. They had not troubled to obtain a licence of marriage, nor had they had the banns called, and the ceremony had taken place at some unknown church, not in the bride's parish church. Jones had posted his caveat, claiming precontract, in Christ Church, where both Milward and Agnes must have seen it. Jones, Field and Flaskett had all duly entered suits in the Ecclesiastical Courts, claiming precontracts, and in the very teeth of all this Milward, a minister and a Doctor of Divinity, had ventured upon a ceremony of marriage with Agnes. By February 1601 all three suits were in full swing, and during the course of these proceedings, a fortnight after Easter in that year, this most improper marriage took place.

It was all very well for Milward, admitting the absence of licence or banns, to argue that he had the approval of Agnes, of Lyde and Kevall, and that he did it only

because he vnderstood by the overseer and disposer of her in marryag by the will of her Aunt That John Howe her father (being a pore man) and having gotten administracion of all her goods, woulde Carrye the same out of the howse of her. . . Aunt, to th vtter vndoing of. . . Agnes, if he had knowne of the. . . marryag,

and further that her mother brought her to be married to him. It was a scandalous proceeding, subversive of all ecclesiastical law, and on the premises the ceremony was invalid.

And so Flaskett immediately set up a new Bill, in which he joined Milward with Agnes, and Field too for good measure, as defendants to his claim of precontract. And the legal pot was fairly set a-boiling.

By this the numerous minor suitors, Povey, Humphrey Rogers, Wright, Cox, Leer, and the rest, had retreated in dismay before these more doughty warriors and left the field clear for them. And they must have lamented their failure considerably the less when they stood by and watched the confused *mêlée* that ensued. The air was cleared, however, before long. Henry Jones, in the Consistory Court of London, was the first to drop out, and he did not even attempt to produce evidence. He let his suit fall. Field went further in the Court of Arches, and Joan Coppians and Agnes Shaw supported his case. But judgment was given against him. And now there remained Flaskett and Milward in single combat *à outrance*. It was a noble battle, with quarter neither given nor taken, while all London, including George Chapman, rejoiced at the spectacle.

Milward took the prudent step of securing Agnes' estate, as far as possible, against possible failure to establish his marriage. For he and Agnes made a deed of gift of her estate to Milward's brother, the Rev. Mathias Milward, Rector of Barnet. This would give Flaskett, if he succeeded, very serious trouble indeed to recover it. Flaskett, justly incensed, spread abroad derogatory stories of past incidents in Milward's career. There was the ugly tale how Milward had been caught out, one day, riding off into Essex with another man's wife. Further, Milward had warned Flaskett and Howe to take heed how they opposed him, bragging that he had ruined one man already, a Cambridgeshire man, who had formerly dared to stand in his way. Finally, Milward himself was no more free than Agnes. For he had had dealings with another Agnes:

Did you not beare Annes the sister of doctor Poape in hand you would Marry her and were you not contracted to her and did not...doctor Poaps sister that night you were marryed to Annes Howe Crye out very grevvsly and was much distempered that the neyghbours were fayne to come to comforte her.

Against such things Milward had a couple of shots in his locker. He had Flaskett arrested for slander, though he let the suit fall, on the advice of his counsel. And he set on his servant, Edward Brampton, to sue Flaskett for a debt of £500 in one of the Courts. The suit failed, but it all incommoded his adversary. Yet these were merely skirmishes in the main action, the course of which was a breathless seesaw. Much money may have changed hands among the interested onlookers, for the Elizabethans were gamblers to a man, and any Londoner would have been justified in backing his fancy on either side.

On the one side was Flaskett, with his solid case, with impregnable evidence of his betrothal, on the strength of the circumstantial accounts of John and Rose Oswald as well as of Flaskett. On the other side was Milward, in possession of Agnes, with her support, and with her denial of precontracts. Moreover, Milward was a Doctor of Divinity, and the case was to be tried by the Ecclesiastical Courts. But he had undoubtedly broken the law and married without licence or banns. And Milward was disadvantageously situated as a result of this. For Flaskett's first blow was a shrewd one. He complained of Milward's marriage to the Court of High Commission, which straightway arrested him, imprisoned him in the Clink, and finally imposed a fine upon him and Agnes. It is Milward himself who tells us how he and Agnes for this offence

> have bin most depelye & grevouslie ponished.

But Agnes stuck to him the more faithfully for this misfortune, and had money and food conveyed to him daily in the Clink during his imprisonment there. It was a very pretty case. And much might depend upon the Judge. It is to be remembered that Dr Dunne was Dean of the Arches, and we have had some taste of his quality.

Here the records of the Court of Delegates furnish full information, a Court of Appeal in respect of such cases as concern Ecclesiastical Courts among others. The case was tried in the Court of Arches, and after hearing it sentence was given by Dr Dunne in favour of Flaskett and of his claim to Agnes. Milward's marriage was declared invalid, as well as irregular.

Milward, however, nothing daunted, appealed to the Court of Delegates. This time Dr Gibson sat as Judge, along with Doctors Legge, Swale and Lloyd. And judgment was given on 20 February 1602, in favour of Milward, with costs. A year later the suit again comes to hearing in the same Court upon a re-trial, by the same bench, except that Sir Julius Caesar took the place of Dr Gibson, and the law veered round once more to Flaskett. Final sentence was given, by which it was ordered that Agnes should be compelled to marry Flaskett, while the pretended marriage with Milward and contract with Field were rejected as null and void. And Agnes was to pay Field's costs in all Courts. The Court evidently held that both Field and Flaskett were injured men, that of the two Flaskett had the prior claim, and that his betrothal was proved to be a binding precontract.

In the meantime, one may well ask, where was Agnes living, and what was she doing? She could not live with Milward, even after he had been liberated from the Clink. Nor could she well be left at the Harrow with her mother and father, in the circumstances. She had to be both protected and guarded, until her matrimonial affairs were settled. It is clear that the Court of Arches, or the Privy Council, provided for her custody, doubtless at the expense of her estate. When Agnes herself appeared in Star Chamber to give evidence, she came in company with Suzan, Countess of Kent,[1] and with Mrs Edith Errington, a widow of good family. Agnes was staying, in fact, in their charge at the Countess of Kent's house at Fulwell Hatch, in Barking, during the trials. Flaskett, as we know, obtained judgment in the end, on 28 February 1603, and the Countess was ordered to deliver Agnes up to Flaskett.

Flaskett went down to Barking early in March 1603, with his order, and had an interview with the Countess, in the presence of Agnes, Mrs Errington, and certain legal gentlemen. He seems to have been indiscreet. Possibly he was so deeply impressed by conversation with a Countess that he inadvertently deviated into candour. Or perhaps, in his hour of triumph, he was simply garrulous.

At any rate, he told them that he had not realized exactly what a contract of marriage was until after he had had an interview with the Archbishop of Canterbury, Whitgift, and related to him what happened between himself and Agnes. His Grace kindly gave him a week to consider the matter. Flaskett went off to consult Dr Crompton, who instructed him that he had a case, whereupon Flaskett pro-

---

[1] The Countess of Kent was a sister of Lord Willoughby. Sir John Wingfield was her first husband. She had had her own troubles, and was involved with the second husband in a dispute about her dowry, which came into Chancery in 1598.

ceeded to sue Agnes in the Arches. Apparently the Countess, advised by George Lymiter, on hearing this, declared that she would not hand Agnes over to him, and Flaskett warned her that he would complain to the Bishop of London, Bancroft. Next morning they all met the Bishop at Fulham Palace, and Lymiter tells us that the Countess made her excuses for not obeying the warrant, and gave her reasons, relating what Flaskett had said the night before. Whereupon Bancroft turned to Flaskett, with a severe question, 'Sirha did you speake thus?' Flaskett sought to explain away his statements. He did not know the significance of the word 'contract', until he saw Dr Crompton. But he knew perfectly well

that a *promise* had so far passed betweene...Agnes and (Flaskett) that (Flaskett) was tied thereby in his Conscience to marrie... Agnes & not anie other woman.

The Bishop then pressed him further. What were the actual words of contract?

    Flaskett   I saied I will have thee to my wife.
    Bishop   These words did not make a contracte.
    Flaskett   But I saied afterwards I doe take thee to my wife.
    Bishop   What was the reason (if you did not know what a contract meant) why you did flie from your first words I will have thee to my wife to the other words I doe take thee to my wife.
    Flaskett   (*No reply.*)
    Bishop (*after a pause*) I perceive your cause is not so cleere as I tooke it to be or as it is thought. I will remember these your words when time shall serve.

And with such an ominous epilogue the Bishop closed the conversation. It is clear that on subsequent enquiry Bancroft learned that further action was contemplated, and so Agnes was allowed to remain with the Countess at Fulwell Hatch, despite the warrant issued as a result of the Delegates' sentence for Flaskett.

Agnes continued in suspense with the Countess, while

Milward brooded for a while over his wrongs, but not without feverish activity, and not as one without hope even now. And on 6 May 1603 he launched a new attack. Despairing of the Ecclesiastical Courts, he turned to Star Chamber by way of an information to Sir Edward Coke, Attorney-General, who prosecuted three considerable groups of defendants, accusing them respectively of conspiracy, perjury, and interference with the course of justice. In the first group were Howe and his friends, with Flaskett; in the second were the witnesses who had given evidence on behalf of Flaskett or Field in the Court of Arches; and in the third we find three persons of the highest interest, a great dramatist, George Chapman, a theatrical speculator, Thomas Woodford, and the manager of a company of actors, Edward Peers, Master of the Children of St Paul's. We may leave for the present the question of their complicity in any conspiracy against Milward, in order to pursue the legal battle to its end.

In the Court of Star Chamber every aspect of the case was exhaustively examined, and a cloud of witnesses were produced on both sides. Milward's case was, in brief, that Howe had corruptly conspired to defraud his daughter, that he had maladministered her estate, and that he had sought to force her into marriage to further his own profit. In this design he had been aided by Peter Howe and his women relatives, excluding his wife. Flaskett had joined in the conspiracy as prospective husband, and had furthermore falsely alleged a betrothal to Agnes, and suborned witnesses to support his claim by perjury in the Ecclesiastical Courts. The Oswalds and Howe's relatives were accused of perjury on behalf of Flaskett and Field respectively.

The usual procedure of Bill and Answers was followed. Henry Jones demurred in law: having dropped his suit and never having produced witnesses, he could not be accused of suborning perjury. The others denied their guilt, in various ways, and the case went on to the taking of evidence on either side, with the interrogation of the defendants, with witnesses in support of the Attorney-General's case, and others brought to testify in Flaskett's favour. The total number of depositions amounted in the end to no less than seventy-one, a formidable pile to disentangle for the Court of Star Chamber, as for the present historian over three hundred years later, when the matter has ceased to interest either the judges, the aggrieved Milward, or the eleven defendants in the case, their busy quarrel long since stilled in a little dust.

Fortunately the evidence can be analysed into certain definite lines of argument, moving in new directions as the case developed. The history of Howe's dealings with his daughter and her estate is reviewed from every possible angle in the search for information, much of which I have already given as set forth by various deponents. One fundamental fact stands out in respect of Flaskett's case for a pre-contract. It was essential, to make his case good, that there should be two credible witnesses to the betrothal other than himself. These were John and Rose Oswald. Without them, or without either of them, his case fell to the ground. For Agnes and Mrs Howe, the only other persons present, denied the contract. But when they were separately interrogated, on 26 May 1603, both stood firmly to a consistent story, which was told in full detail. Both had been present at the betrothal, and both had seen and heard the proceedings. Rose is particularly hard pressed on various crucial points. Did she know of the betrothal of her own knowledge and in her own hearing? Where, and when, did it take place? Who was present? Was it conditional or absolute? Did Agnes and Flaskett give each other their hands? And what were the precise actual words of contract spoken? There are odd moments in Rose's evidence. Having recited her story, she adds that she

for her owne parte was vnwilling to have discovered (these words of contract) but her husband... would needes haue her to depose them bycause she had hard them spoken.

Indeed, but for her husband's wishes she would willingly have concealed the truth thereof. It might seem that Rose was faltering. But her evidence could not be got over. Attempts were made, of course, to discredit them. Was not Oswald a very poor man? Oswald replies

that he doth live by his trade & is not a verie poore man for he is worthe one hundred marks his detts being paied.

If he were very poor, it follows that he would be amenable to bribery and so easily led to perjury. Rose is more truthful here, perhaps. For she admits that John 'is but a poor man, yet not indebted but for tryfles'. But she denies all undue influence, and holds fast to her story. And at this stage, on 26 May 1603, Flaskett had won all along the line. He had his judgment in the Delegates Court, and the Court of Star Chamber could not but uphold it, as things stood. Milward and Agnes were about to be separated for good. And Agnes would be compelled by order of law to implement a binding contract with Flaskett by the further ceremony of marriage in church. Milward has made his last cast, in vain.

Then, suddenly, came the last and most dramatic turn of the tide, to Flaskett a thundercloud overshadowing a beauteous day, to Milward 'a jewel hung in ghastly night'. A memorandum is noted among the depositions in Star Chamber, dated 4 July 1603:

Memorandum. that...Rose Oswald the daie and year abovesaid came before William Mill Esqr Clarke of his Maiesties Councell and with teares & gryef of conscyenc voluntarily confessed & acknowledged that where she had lately in the Corte of Starr Chamber in her examinacion taken at the suite of his Maiesty's Attorney generall affyrmed and sayd vppon her othe that she had in her owne howse heard a Contract of marriage betwixt John fflaskett & Agnes Howe (as in her sayd examinacion nowe again reade vnto her appeareth) the truth was that in that poynt of her examinacion she had to th offence of god & her conscyence falsely vntrewely forsworne herself for that in very truthe she dyd not heare the same contracte as she had deposed

but that she had byn tolde by her husband & by fflaskett that they
vppon their othes had deposed that theire was such a contracte
betwixt fflaskett & Agnes & that therefore she might allso depose
the same contracte which speeches of her husband & of fflaskett
moved her to take vppon her so to depose in her examinacion
as she hath doune, for the which her offence She is most hartily
sorry & humbly submitteth her self to the Commiseracion of this
honourable Corte & allso besecheth Mr doctor Millward & suche
others as by her false othe sworn may be wronged & paenalized
to forgyve her. And lastly & especyally with most humble &
hartie teares desireth allmighty god of his goodnes & mercy to
forgyve her. In wyttnes whereof she hath herunto before the
Clarke of the Councell sett her hand.

This was a catastrophic performance, which changed the
whole aspect of things. For the keystone of Flaskett's case
had dropped out when Rose Oswald's support was removed.
Incidentally, she had in effect turned King's evidence against
her husband too. What John Oswald thought of his wife's
confession when he knew of it, we hear a week after, in the
evidence of George Howe, on 14 July. Howe was at the
Oswalds' house on Friday, 8 July, and

then found that there was some variaunce betwene...John
Oswald & Rose his wife...Oswald being much offended with
her & calling her whore because she had lately before (as he saied)
confessed before Mr Mill clerke of the Starr-chamber that she
had forsworne herself in her examinacion there lately before
taken,...Oswald then also saieing to his...wife that she had so
confessed herself to be forsworne by the meanes of Doctor
Milwards man for fear or for some guifts or promise made or
given to her by...Dr Milwards man...Wherevnto...Rose
presently aunswered bitterly weepinge to her husband with these
words viz you will needs be a Ruler in your owne house you
should have ruled me in honest things you say that I have vndone
you but you have vndone me & yourself to in overuling of me
in that which was not honest & so have not only cast away your
owne soule but made me to damne myne to & to sweare that
which I never knewe nor sawe.

As long as she lived in this world, she said to Howe with

weeping tears and making great moan, she would never go back on her confession, which had relieved her disquiet mind. And then, Howe continues

Rose taking a cuppe with drinke into her hande saied to... John Oswald...I drinke to you John Oswald, husband And presently therevpon...John Oswald in discontented manner vttred these words viz drinke to mine eares whoore for I have eares now & might have had still if thou haddest not ben a whoore, but hereafter I shall have none & that very shortly too.

I cannot tell whether Oswald lost his ears or not.[1] But he had abandoned hope too soon. For Rose's confession was deeply impugned at once. New troops were rushed into the yawning breach in Flaskett's case. On the one hand they sought to prove, with circumstantial evidence, that Milward was at the bottom of Rose's change of front, and that his servant, Edward Brampton, had taken the extremest steps to persuade Rose to confess falsely. The volume of such evidence is considerable, and not to be dismissed lightly. And Brampton, who describes himself as a Merchant Adventurer, was a queer sort of servant for Dr Milward to have. The fact is, I am sure, that Milward armed himself, for the purpose of his struggle in law, with an old hand at crooked and unscrupulous dealings, a kind of private detective, of the brotherhood of London sharks like Marlowe's friends Pooley and Skeres. John Hardie, a Stationer, and his wife Margery were most helpful. Hardie related that after her confession Rose had told him that her confession was false and was extorted from her:

she was drawn to make the same confession...by the lewde meanes & practyce of one Brampton doctor Mylwards man who in such sorte had terrifyed her husband by causing of the Warden

---

[1] He was certainly in financial trouble in March 1603, when he owed the Stationers' Company £2, and was raising a loan of £8 from them on the security of the lease of his house. (*Records of the Court of the Stationers' Company*, p. 93.)

of the ffleets man to goe aboute to apprehende him to have him
in the ffleete & so to vndoe him being a poore man as that hee
durst not to goe abrode to gett in his worke for his mayneteyn-
inge & lyving as he was woont to doe & by theise meanes...John
Oswalde her husbande fell into...great wantes.

Brampton, with the help of certain women, and by dint of
promising Rose that she and her husband would be set free
and clear of all the legal pother in which they were involved,
if she would retract her first evidence, at last drew Rose to
her confession, in the hope of peace and safety. I cannot go
into further details of Brampton's devices with Rose, but
they would furnish a few admirable scenes of a Middleton
comedy.

On the other hand, the relative credibility of John and
Rose Oswald obviously became a burning question. And
a platoon of Oswald's fellow-Stationers was doubled up to
testify to his probity. Among them were some notable
names, for the list of them includes Vincent Williamson,
John Jaggard, the first John Harrison, John Hardie, Laurence
Lysle, and Felix Norton. All depose that Oswald has been
a good servant to the Stationers' Company, and has made an
honest living by his trade as a bookbinder. Moreover, they
defend him against the accusation of drunkenness, though
old John Harrison qualifies his testimony: he

hath seene...Oswalde many tymes merry with drincke, but
never sawe him very druncke to his knowledge.

Lysle also has seen him merry, but never absolutely overcome with drink. Rose herself was asked whether John was
given to swearing, and whether during the last four or five
years he has often come home drunk and very unruly and
has beaten her and shut her out of doors. Her stammering
reply, faithfully noted verbatim by the clerk, reveals her
painful embarrassment:

To the 8 Inte...[she sayth]...[besecheth the hono]...[an-
sweth not]...[desierth she] humbly besecheth this honourable
Court she may not be inforced to answere.

Milward's witnesses are less hesitant. According to Brampton, Oswald was not only a common drunkard and a most horrible swearer, but a lewd liver, who

> was and is taken for a verie poore and beggarlie fellow, and of no reputacion or creditt, but taken for a knight of the poast or common baile.

John Webster describes him as

> a verye poore man and ys very often drunke, and a very great swerer, and...for a smale Consideracion will swere any thinge, and...by his owne Reporte att seuerall tymes...hathe byne a verye vicious & lewde lyver of his bodye & ys of verye smale Creditt in the parishe where he dwells, and this deponent knoweth not any man that will trust him for 12*d*.

It is alleged that he is often to be seen 'druncke and reeling in the streetes', so much so that it is 'a common saying of him passing in the streetes There goes drunken Oswald'. And I am afraid that his brother-Stationers went as far as they dared to mitigate the truth in this respect.

Flaskett, in turn, deals some shrewd blows at Milward's helpers and witnesses, as for example in the comments of Margery Hardie. Agnes Blundell is 'A woman of contentious and lewde behauiour & one that hath been comytted to Brydewell for ill behauiour'. Grace Page was carted 'in Somer last was xij monthes'. Ellen Reed, four years ago, was committed to Bridewell. Richard Harlowe was guilty of unmentionable things, was long a prisoner in the Counter, and died in the Hole there. He and Willsher, says John Hardie, were notorious shifters and cony-catching fellows, who undid many honest men, and sold counterfeit gold and silver quills. Willsher subsequently fled the country. Yet Dr Milward had people like Agnes Blundell to dine with him, a virago whose husband, a Stationer, complains of her ill usage of him, driving him from his house, bed and board, and forcing him to work elsewhere. What could Milward and Brampton be doing with such people, except hatching evil plots against Rose and her husband and Flaskett?

It is, I think, impossible to conceive a more tangled web of sturdy swearing on both sides to a more bewildering mass of detailed circumstance. The judges in the Star Chamber had not even, as a rule, the opportunity of seeing the witnesses and of measuring their character. Most of the evidence came to them only in written depositions, though they could, and did occasionally, call a witness before them for a personal hearing. It was amazingly difficult for them to arrive at the truth. My own impression is that Agnes did in fact take part in conversations amounting to a formal betrothal with both Field and Flaskett, that Rose was not in fact present at the betrothal with Flaskett, though she was in the house and knew that it was taking place, and that Milward and Brampton did in fact play upon her fears and hopes to lead her to her confession, and went to all lengths to bring it about. I believe that Agnes never liked Field and was forced into the ceremony with him. I feel sure that her first inclination, as with Mrs Howe, was to accept Flaskett as a suitable husband, but that when the hitherto unapproachable, imposing figure of the Preacher at Christ Church descended from the pulpit and presented himself as a suitor, Agnes was greatly impressed by the reverend Cophetua, and also judged that he with his powerful connections would solve her problem and provide her with a safe refuge as well as a place in superior society beyond all her hopes.

As for the Court, surely they could not fail to be influenced by Agnes' own evidence that she had, in fact, never betrothed herself to Flaskett. She had been with the Countess of Kent long enough for the Countess to judge of her probity and to give her opinion accordingly to the Judges. The Bishop of London, again, would be consulted, and we have seen how suspicious he was of Flaskett's case. Finally, Milward was, after all, a Doctor of Divinity, and a notable preacher, who was soon to receive clear marks of royal favour. The balance of influence, as well as the balance of expediency, was in Milward's favour. And the Court decided accordingly. The only evidence of its decision is to be found in subsequent events, but it is clear. The last depositions in Star Chamber were taken in February 1604. And on 30 May 1604 the King ordered a Commission of Review in the case of Dr Milward and his wife Agnes against Flaskett, to consider the sentence of Sir Julius Caesar in the Court of Delegates. A formidable Court was constituted, with Toby Mathew, Bishop of Durham, Ridley, Popham, Anderson and Bruce. Milward's appeal succeeded, Caesar's sentence was reversed, the marriage was declared legitimate, and Flaskett was condemned to costs in the action, when judgment was promulgated on 12 November. And the destination of Agnes and her fortune, or what was left of it, was at last settled for good, after four full years of swaying fortunes. It is difficult to think of a more cruel ordeal for a decent girl to undergo between the ages of sixteen and twenty.

She had been dragged through the Ecclesiastical Courts and through the Court of Star Chamber. And her father had seen to it that her affairs came also before the Court of Chancery, in which Howe complained upon Dr Milward, alleging in effect a series of thefts both of the property of Margaret Sharles and of Howe's private property from the Harrow, in collusion with the Lydes. Depositions were taken in October 1604, shortly before the Commission of Review put an end to Flaskett's short-lived triumph, in November. It is clear from certain Decrees and Orders that Milward replied by a counter-suit a few months later, when his position had been immeasurably strengthened by this turn of the wheel of fortune, and that Howe was hard put to it to answer to the joint Bill of Milward and Agnes. The Court unsympathetically rejected his attempt to quash it by a Demurrer, and two further attempts to answer were both adjudged insufficient. Beyond this no information is available, and the outcome of these suits is not recorded. They probably petered out.

Elizabeth Abbott, the maidservant who brought news of

the pursuivants, reappeared to give evidence. She had remained with Agnes after her marriage with Milward and the eviction of Howe from the Harrow. She agreed that Milward took possession of all he found there, including all household stuff and most of Mrs Sharles' wares and glass, on the very day of his marriage, about six months after the death of Mrs Sharles. Lyde, the minister of Christ Church, and his wife Sibill, both depose. Lyde was then aged seventy-two and Sibill 'sixty and upwards'. Lyde relates how Mrs Sharles' valuables, plate and papers, were locked up in a large trunk, with four locks, so that it could be opened only by the joint action of the four holders of keys, Nicholas Fuller, a Reader of Gray's Inn, Lyde, Kevall the scrivener and joint overseer of the will with Lyde, and Howe. For further safety the trunk was laid in a room with two locks, to which Lyde and Howe held the keys. But Howe made light of these elaborate precautions, and simply broke open door and trunk alike, and then did what he pleased. Both Lyde and Sibill defend themselves against Howe's accusation that they had shared in the loot, and there is a touch of pathos in the old lady's complaint that Howe is trying to catch her out, as no doubt he was, by repeating questions put to her three years before:

She is sure that the Complainant (having molested her in divers Courts she knoweth not in how many nor where) did once or twice minister this or the like article vnto her, to which she then answered and referreth her selfe to that her answere, the rather for that her memory now fayleth her, and then thes questions now asked were such as she remembered a more certen answere to them, then now she can.

Having achieved this involved piece of syntax, she appends her straggling cross to her deposition, and makes a protesting escape from her persistent persecutor. Howe evidently had called Henry Squire, a former servant of Mrs Sharles, with interrogatories ready for him to aver that Lyde had made £500 out of her estate. But Squire failed to appear, and we must hope for the best concerning the minister. What stands out most clearly from these depositions is the faithfulness of Agnes to Milward, once she had become his wife. For it is here that Elizabeth Abbott tells us how Agnes saw to his welfare when he was lying prisoner in the Clink. Whatever was taken to him there, food or drink or comforts, was done—Elizabeth is sure of this—by the orders of Agnes herself. We cannot tell what her first thoughts may have been concerning Flaskett as a possible husband. But she had now set up her rest, for better or for worse, and was no fair weather wife to Milward.

The married life of Milward and Agnes was of no long duration, though not without every sign of contentment as long as it lasted. They continued to live in Margaret Sharles' house, the Harrow in Newgate Market, and Milward officiated as Preacher at Christ Church until his death. Three children, however, were born to them during this short period, James, Mary and Margaret, due deference being paid in the first and last of these names to the authors of their fortunes. For Milward was made a Chaplain to King James, and was even chosen to preach one of the annual sermons upon the deliverance of the King from the Gowry conspiracy, on 5 August 1607, an occasion of which Milward made the most, with a profusion of learning in Latin, Greek and even Hebrew.

In April 1609 Milward was sent by the King on a mission to Scotland, with a hundred marks in his pocket for his expenses, paid over to him on 15 April. Recognizing the perils of such a venture, he made his will, on 10 April, somewhat hurriedly, because of his

greate busines in this suddain appoyntment & expedition by his maiestie into Scotland.

His forebodings were prophetic, for the expedition in fact proved fatal to him, and he died, according to Anthony Wood, on 1 August. According to his brother Mathias, he

had found good friends at Edinburgh, in particular the Lord
Treasurer of Scotland, in whose house he died despite all the
'cost and skill, paines and praiers' lavished upon him. The
Earl of Dunbar bestowed upon him a 'sumptuous Funerall',
and upon his servants 'large remuneration', in token of his
esteem, and further persuaded the King to grant an annuity
of a hundred pounds sterling to his wife and children. Here
was some consolation for the 'life fraught with crosses'
which, as Mathias saw it, were to fit him for that heavenly
Jerusalem of which he 'dead is now an euerlasting stone'.
And here was proof of the favour of his earthly master who,
again in the words of Mathias,

did out of his Heroick and Princely clemency, a compassionate
pitier of wrong'd simplicity, rescue him from the jawes of conspiring perjurie.

His will was proved by Agnes on 29 August. There is
perhaps some unusual significance in the clause wherein
Milward 'forgives all that have offended him in word or
deed'. He left the Harrow and other houses, once Mrs
Sharles', 'to Agnes my loving and most faythfull wief', a
phrase that compares perhaps characteristically with the
humbler William Sharles' more kindly and affectionate
tribute to 'my well-beloved wife Margaret'. Agnes was to
hold them for life, and thereafter they went to his son and
heir James. His manuscripts of sermons and the like he left
to his brother Mathias, the Rector of Barnet, who ventured
in 1610 upon printing the Gowry sermon under the title of
Jacobs Great Day of Trouble, and Deliverance. The sermon
shows us the Doctor of Divinity with full sail set, on his own
great day, now with pomp and parade of learning, now
peremptory with righteous venom, now exuding the oil of
adulation, and now unbending with ungainly playfulness of
puns and other facetious figures of the lower rhetoric, in a
complete display of his professional powers. Despite this,
however, Mathias, whose heavily witty address to the reader

envisages further ventures, was evidently not encouraged
to proceed, and published no more memorials of his distinguished brother. His lengthy *Epistle Dedicatorie* to the
Earl of Dunbar furnishes us with some of the facts concerning
Milward's death. And Patrick Sands of Edinburgh ('Patricius
ab Arenis Edinburgensis') not only salutes the dead in two
Latin epigrams, but also confirms, or rather provides, the
date of death stated by Anthony Wood.

Milward may have been a Hertfordshire man, for he held
property in Hertford which did not come from Agnes. But
his parents, who survived him, owned land in Sutton in
Surrey. He was thirty-eight years of age on 28 July 1603,
when he gave evidence, and was therefore born in 1564–5.
(A John Milward from Derbyshire, of Broadgates Hall,
formerly of Christ Church, was admitted M.A. in 1584,
having matriculated in 1581, at the age of 25. This could not
be our Doctor.) It is possible that he was the John Milward
who married Mary Blounte at St Clement Danes on 20
November 1591, and that Agnes was his second wife.

One of Milward's witnesses in his long suits, Agnes Evans,
a Newgate girl, was amply rewarded for her faithfulness, for
his brother the Rector married her on 28 March 1605.
Flaskett continued to exercise his trade, as the records of the
Stationers' Company bear witness. Concerning Henry
Jones, his first rival, I know nothing further. As for the ill-
used Field, he crops up again in the Court of Requests in
1617, seeking to arrange proceedings in bankruptcy. For
Field is indebted in the amount of £750, and is reduced to
selling his lands. And here we have the final echo of our
story, until its present resurrection. For Field attributes his
failure to the enormous costs of his suit against Agnes and
Milward, into which, he maintains, Howe persuaded him to
enter. Furthermore, Howe promised Field to meet all the
costs of the action, if it cost £500, but in the end 'payd not
one groat' though Field sought payment from him. Finally,
Howe even now claims a debt of fifty pounds from Field,

instead of paying the £500 he ought 'in conscions...to make recompence' to Field. And so, eight years after Milward has died, old John Howe is no less active and busy, with his harpy claws still firmly embedded in Field. I can only add that Field had long since ceased to mourn the loss of Agnes, and had consoled himself with another wife.

I am obliged to record further that in the very year of publication of Milward's Gowry sermon, a year after his death, Agnes provided his children with a protector and herself with a second husband. In 1610 she was married at Milward's church, Christ Church, Newgate, to Thomas Proud, Vicar of Enfield. She had, at any rate, kept to the cloth.

§ iv. THE PLAY AT ST PAUL'S

So in the end the story leaves Dr John Milward, the ultimate winner of Agnes Howe's hand and estate, in his grave after a fatal visit to Scotland, Agnes safe at Enfield with her three children, mistress of the Vicarage of that pleasant country town, within easy reach of Mathias and his wife at Barnet, Jones lost to view but probably back in Gloucester, Flaskett a busy stationer, Field in the throes of bankruptcy, and John Howe still clutching at him in his ruin in 1617. In the interval between this time and the exciting events which ended thus, many no less wonderful happenings had intervened, for example the notorious scandal of the divorce of the Earl of Essex, the consequent poisoning of Sir Thomas Overbury by the means of the Countess of Essex, and the sensational sequel of her trial, along with her new husband, the Earl of Somerset, the King's own especial favourite, for murder. The citizens thus had other things to talk about. For the lawyers, *lassati, nondum satiati*, there were still pickings. But the affairs of Agnes Howe and her marriage soon receded into oblivion, and remained undisturbed for three hundred years, to be disinterred for the sake of a minor and unimportant episode in the complex interplay of so many persons and so many motives of action.

It is time to turn to this aspect of the story, which is unfolded, along with the rest, in the far-reaching survey of events in the proceedings of Star Chamber. Our first information that Agnes Howe's affairs offer literary interest comes from the Attorney-General's Bill. It is alleged against Flaskett that, not content to conspire against Agnes by means of false evidence in the Ecclesiastical Courts, he also arranged during the very course of the trial

that a stage play should be made & was made by one George Chapman vpon a plott given vnto him concerning...Agnes Howe...(her cause & sutes then depending) & the same vnder coulorable & fayned names personated, so made & contryved was sold to Thomas Woodford & Edward Pearce for xx marks to be played vpon the open stages in diuers play houses within the citie of London to resemble and publish the dealing of her father towards her concerning his practize with seuerall sutors to bestow her in marriage with one that might forgoe her portion & that therbie she might shutt vp & conclude a match with... fflaskett rather then to suffer her name to be so traduced in euery play house as it was lyke to be.

Having made these arrangements along with his preparation of false evidence on the part of the Oswalds, Flaskett continued with his suit, produced his witnesses, and followed up with the stage-play:

And the...confederates after the...false oathes & depositions made as aforesaid & before the sentence given caused the stage play...to be made and played for that purpose aboue specifyed during all the last Hillarie terme vntill the very daie wherein sentence should be giuen in that...cause & vpon the very same daie also.

The terms of this accusation are clear enough. It was Flaskett's scheme to intimidate Agnes into marrying him, in order to avoid scandal. To this end he went to a dramatist of his acquaintance, Chapman. Chapman was in the first flight of dramatists, and any play by him would find its market with one or other of the companies of actors, and would attract attention when produced on the stage. Flaskett prepared for Chapman the requisite material in the shape of a plot, giving a summary of the situation and of the story of Howe's negotiations with the various suitors. Chapman agreed to his proposals and got to work on the play. Flaskett then returned to Agnes and threatened her with the prospect of her public shame in the pillory of a public stage, as well as with the case he had bolstered up with the evidence of the Oswalds. Agnes stood firm, nevertheless, and Flaskett went on to fulfil his threats. The play was finished by Chapman, who sold it to Thomas Woodford and Edward Peers for twenty marks, evidently to be performed by the Children of St Paul's, of whom Peers was then Master. And throughout the course of the appeal in the Court of Delegates it was acted at St Paul's right up to the day when judgment was to be given. It is clearly implied that not only did Flaskett fulfil his threat to Agnes, but he intended the play to arouse public interest, to present his case outside the Court as well as in it, and in a measure to attempt to influence the Court to its decision. The Court, in fact, gave sentence in favour of Flaskett, on 28 February 1603.

So Chapman, Woodford and Peers were proceeded against as aiding and abetting Flaskett and his other confederates in their conspiracy against Agnes. It is noteworthy that they are not accused of libelling Agnes or her father or Milward. This accusation was quite specifically made against Dekker and Rowley and Aaron Holland in 1623 in respect of their play *Keep the Widow Waking*. We may not, however, assume that no case lay for such an accusation here, and that the play was innocuous or remote from the facts and persons of the story. It is evident that the main butt of the play was John Howe, in fact. And John Howe was a defendant in this suit along with Chapman and the others. This alone would spike the guns of any libel action.

Subpoenas were duly served upon our three men of the theatre. Chapman was the first to appear to swear his Answer to the Bill, on 19 May 1603. His Answer is elusive and devoid of information:

touchinge any Combinacions or Confederacyes vpon a plott to him giuen by any of the...defendants or any other person or persons what soeuer to make any suche stage playe to be played vpon the open stages in diuerse Play Howses within the Citye of London to resemble and publishe the dealinge of...John How towards...Anne Howe...concerninge...John Howes practise with seuerall Suters to bestowe her in Marriadge...he...saeith that he is not therof nor any parte therof guilty.

His lawyer, William Knaplocke, who drew up and signed his Answer, saw the loopholes in the accusation, which left Chapman free to deny any conspiratorial action, and to deny having received a plot from Flaskett or anybody, without touching upon the more delicate question whether he had written such a play or sold it, a question which he quite legitimately evades. Next came Thomas Woodford, on 23 May, who runs to greater length and detail in his Answer. First he protests against the whole case, which is due to the 'sinister relation' of Milward, and only intended to trouble and molest good citizens like himself. Further, it is clearly a matter for the Ecclesiastical Courts, and should be left to them, as they are busy with it already. He himself has nothing to do with the matrimonial problems of Agnes, and of all the persons involved knows only Peers and Chapman, and Flaskett slightly. As for the specific matter alleged in Star Chamber, he gives a full reply and carries the war into the enemy's camp:

true it is that he bought one playe booke of...George Chapman beinge Lycencede by the Mr of our Layte Soueringe Lady the quenes maiestyes Revels he not knowing that yt touchede any person lyvinge and further...sayethe that the...playe booke was played by the children of powles in a pryvate house of a longe tyme keepte vsed & accustomede for yt purpose whervnto Re-

queste was made by doctor Whyte one of the Mrs of the churche
of Powles...by the speciall procurement of...doctor Milwarde
to surcease or forbeare the playinge of the playe for that as this
Defendante then did take yt...Doctor Milwarde through his
Jelious consceynce erroniouslye pretendede yt to concerne him
and his cause in the arches betwne him and others whom he was
then in sute with for a woman then by him pretended to be his
wife, wherevppon Edwarde Peerce one of the defendantes...not
only in satisfaction of the...doctors gyltie conscience or Jeliouse
mynde...but also clearly to take awaye his erronious conceyte
therein deliuered the...booke to the...doctor to pervse ouer
who had and deteynde the same for the space of two weakes...
& then redeliuered the same booke to this Defendante at which
tyme he declared in the heringe & presents of dyvers credible
persons that there was note anythinge in the...playe booke that
touchede him at all.

Woodford is ready to prove all this. And he continues with
a denial of any charge that a play was made concerning Agnes
and her affairs and her lawsuits, as far as his knowledge went,
a saving clause that was capable of the most elastic interpretation. Probably his counsel, Thomas Barton, made him
add this paragraph to his gratifyingly profuse detail concerning the play that Milward made such an absurd fuss about.

Finally, on 7 June, Edward Peers appeared. His Answer
showed that he felt himself to be very comfortably situated
in respect of such a charge, for it verges on the impertinent:

Wheras...it is layd for a great offence against this defendant
that a certeine play-booke Mencyoned vnder straunge tearmes
in the...Bill of Complaint was soulde vnto one Thomas Wood-
forde and this Defendant for twenty markes, this Defendant as
to this sayeth, That he neyther boughte the...playbooke neyther
doth hee att any tyme disbourse anye money for buyeinge the
playes which vsually are acted by the Children of Powles, but his
care is otherwyse ymployed for the Educacion of the...Childrene
and to instructe them as apperteyneth to his place and Charge,
And therfore yf it shalbe thoght an offence by this honorable
Courte to buy a play-booke in this manner this Defendant...is
not guiltye.

Nor is he guilty of any conspiracy or subornation of perjury. Therefore he, like Chapman and Woodford, urges that he should be dismissed from the case and granted his costs in the matter. The Court, however, could not fail to perceive the general evasiveness of these Answers, whether couched in the terse cautiousness of Chapman, the loquacious protestations of Woodford, or the contemptuous confidence of Peers. For all three in due course were called before the Court to be interrogated upon their respective shares in the production of the play. Most of the other defendants, and certain witnesses also, were questioned either upon their complicity therein, or upon their presence at the acting of the play and their impressions of it.

Chapman's own evidence is, of course, of the highest interest, and yields a great deal of information. He was, it seems, further examined on 30 May, when he was taken through a series of interrogatories. He admits that he

did heare it reported by a generall reporte that there was a Suit in the Ecclesiasticall Courte betwene a Doctor & one fflaskett & a barbers daughter for marriage,

but he cannot remember details of how he came to hear of it. It is true that

he did make a stage Play called the old Joyner of Algate & that he finisshed the same presently after christmas last And...that no person or persons did advise this defendant thervnto neither had this (*defendant* omitted) instruccion in that matter by anie person by writinge nor otherwise but this defendant made the same of his owne invention.

This is his answer to the direct suggestion that someone

delivered ytt to you...in writtinge in waye of a plott or by private conference.

We should not, I think, take the word *plot* here in its technical sense, to mean the skeleton of a play prepared for the stage, wanting only the dialogue, or the scenario of a play as it means in the case of *Keep the Widow Waking* or in various instances in Henslowe's *Diary*. It is probably used in the vaguer sense of the story to be utilized in the construction of a play. But it is not impossible that a man like Flaskett should have thought of trying his hand at setting forth his story in dramatic form, selecting the scenes that seemed to him fit for a comedy. There was authority for a Stationer turning dramatist, in the persons of Anthony Munday and Henry Chettle.

The play was, however, a private venture of Chapman, and of his own invention, based upon such information as was common knowledge concerning the facts of the case. The date of its composition is precisely indicated. It was finished soon after Christmas 1602. This is obviously an important fact. For it means that the actual history available to serve as a basis for Chapman's play included Milward's successful first appeal to the Court of Delegates, but ended before Flaskett's reversal of that judgment in the later sentence of the Court in February 1603.

Chapman next tells us that, having so written the play, he sold it to Woodford for twenty marks ($£13. 6s. 8d.$), and therefore made so much profit by his venture. But he indicates clearly the total absence of any subsequent interest in this nursling of his Muse, to such a degree indeed that he

never sawe the same acted & plaied publiquely vpon a stage.

It is well to beware of Elizabethan evidence, in respect both of *suppressio veri* and *suggestio falsi*, as well as of more flagitious false gods. It is difficult to believe that Chapman never went to see his play acted. And it may be that the emphasis in his statement should be heavily laid upon the final four words, which were an addition interlined. The publicity of the insult was the onus of the accusation and the words 'publiquely vpon a stage' may well be Chapman's saving clause here. Woodford, it may be observed, is careful to insist that the play was acted 'in a pryvate house' and not in a public theatre. The distinction between the two classes of theatres,

indicated by these adjectives, was very misleading, for public
and private theatres were at this time at least equally open
to spectators on payment. But evidently it could still be
urged in a court of law that the distinction was valid. If
Chapman in fact never visited Paul's house to see the play
acted, his neglect could only be interpreted as a sign of contempt for his own work, as hackwork forced upon him by
the necessity of turning an honest penny by his trade. It is
true that elsewhere in Chapman's work we find evidence
that he caught up into his plays current matter of notorious
interest, as in *Eastward Ho!*, *Monsieur d'Olive* or *Sir Giles
Goosecap*, all written for the Children of Blackfriars. But
nowhere except in *The Old Joiner of Aldgate* did he take the
whole plot of a play from such a source, as far as we know.

Chapman goes on to deny, nevertheless, that any 'particular person' told him that he recognized the story of Agnes
and her suitors in *The Old Joiner of Aldgate*, and to a further
question replies:

that he was not [directed] told of manie things misliked in the
Play and had the same to be corrected...but...heard that some
[generall] excepcions were taken to some parts of the Play but
he never had the same to be corrected neither did make anie
Prologue reprehending them that found fault therewith...And
further...he hath heard it reported that a Doctor of Powles did
entreate or speake to haue the Play forborne to be plaied for 4 or
5 daies but otherwise...doth not know that the same was for-
bidden to be plaied [nor the cause why it was inhibited].

He never to his remembrance heard

anie of the Poets & Plaiers say that they that hindered it were
better they had not done it for there was a Prologue |made which
would nerely touch them.

It is clear from this that Dr Milward heard enough about the
play to know that it was a close reflection of the events in
which he was concerned, that he was able to bring influence
to bear to have the play suspended for a time for enquiry,

that he failed to have it prohibited altogether, and that the play was resumed after a short interval.

We may well ask why a Doctor of Paul's was called in and had the power to inhibit the play or to influence the company. It is clear that the Cathedral clergy retained a greater measure of control over the Children of Paul's than one is apt to realize at this stage in the career of the company. It would seem that the Children continued to be organized as pupils of the Song School of St Paul's, with a Master appointed by the Chapter, though they were in effect a company of professional actors, and that they used for their performances rooms within the precincts of the Cathedral and under its control. I shall return to the Children and their Master in connection with the question of the disposal of Chapman's play to them.

Chapman is further asked concerning a supposed second part of the play or revised version:

haue you A true Coppye of the first . . . whether haue you altered ytt since the firste playeinge therof,

and replies

that he hath not made a second parte therof nor hath anie Copie of the . . . first stage Play neither did alter anie parte thereof since the first plaieng therof.

The suggestion made here is that, while the play as originally written was licensed by the Master of the Revels and so was unassailable, it was subsequently revised and made more offensive. And Chapman, in replying, makes it clear that his autograph manuscript of the play, the only copy he made, went to Woodford, and that he, having so sold it, in effect washed his hands of it and had no further dealings with it. To a further question concerning the history of the play he replies that before he wrote it he knew Howe by sight. He had not heard from any particular person the story of his dealings with suitors, but knew it by general report. And here his first statement reported as common knowledge that

Howe 'had sold...his daughter' to be contracted to several persons. This was deleted immediately, leaving a simple reference to Agnes' various contracts and to the subsequent lawsuits. Chapman then goes on:

before christmas last past...Woodford cominge to me & being then acquainted that I was abouts a Play called the Old Joyner of Algate, I then told...Woodford that he should haue the same Play of me when it was finisshed & so I then sold the same to... Woodford but did not finishe it vntill after christmas last & then I deliuered the same out of my hands.

And now Chapman is asked about the capital question of the characters of the play, and replies:

that in the...stage Play there was a Barber & others personated or plaied viz The barber called Snapper, his daughter called Lady Daughter by the name of Vrsula & others by other names mencioned in the Play.

But by no means did he enter into any conspiracy with the intent

by or vnder color of the said names to shame or disgrace... Agnes How, her ffather & others her sutors,

nor did he ever before the present suit hear of Field or of Humphrey of the Court, to his remembrance. Finally, as far as he knows, none of the defendants, Flaskett, Field or Oswald, or anyone else, instigated either the writing or the acting of the play. Nor was Chapman ever told that any matter in the play had been put into it to slander Agnes, Flaskett, Field, Jones, Joan Daniell or Coppians, or Humphrey Rogers (Humphrey of the Court) under 'Bye names' or stage names. The suggestion here seems to be that even if Chapman wrote the play in an inoffensive form, it might have been revised, after Woodford had bought it, to give it a more direct relation to the persons of the story.

This concluded Chapman's examination, from which it is clear that he refused absolutely to admit complicity in any conspiracy to libel Agnes and the others. But nowhere is he asked point blank whether his play had in fact any basis, either in action or in characters, in the story of Agnes Howe and her suitors.

It is evident, even from Chapman's meagre account of the characters, that he could hardly have denied this. Other evidence is at hand to supplement his account, from which we can reconstruct the principal *dramatis personae*, as follows:

Snipper Snapper. A Barber (John Howe).
Ursula or Lady Daughter. Daughter to Snipper Snapper (Agnes Howe).
Mrs Glasbie. Aunt to Ursula (Mrs Margaret Sharles).
Tresacres. Suitor to Ursula (Field).
Touchbox. Suitor to Ursula (Flaskett).
Umphrevile. Suitor to Ursula (Humphrey Rogers, Humphrey of the Court).
A French Doctor. Suitor to Ursula (Dr Milward).
Spitter Spatter (John Oswald?).
Other Suitors (Jones, Wright, Cox, Leer, etc.?).

With such a list, one can only marvel at the effrontery, or the sophistry, of Flaskett when he informed the Court that he could not say, on his oath, that these stage characters represented any of the real persons in question. Doubtless he could justify himself. The stage characters varied from any possible originals. Or he was perhaps a precursor of a fashionable modern school of criticism. It was not for him to take upon himself to peer into the secret places of Chapman's mind, or to stain the white radiance of his art with the shadows of his environment. Indeed, when Flaskett went to see the play acted, he did not, he says,

make anie regarde or accounte of the same but as Toys & iests such as are acted in other Places.

But the evidence is overwhelming. Edward Brampton, Milward's man, also saw the play, and fully understood that it gave a clear reflection of the actual persons and events. Moreover, Brampton met and talked with Woodford, who told him that it was indeed so. Finally, 'it is a common

report in the towne that it is so'. The fullest account of the
origin and significance of the play is given by Woodford,
and some of his remarks lead us to reconsider Chapman's
account in one respect. Woodford is curiously inconclusive
concerning the first stage in the manufacture of the play. He
admits, being questioned on this point, that

he did once say there was a plott of the...Play delivered vnto
Chapman but...doth not know who delivered that Plott nor
whether there was anie Plott delivered to him or not &...that
for anie thinge this defendant knoweth the...Play was conceived
& contrived by Chapman onely.

He is then asked whether he had said that

fflaskett made the Plott of the...playe, was yt not full and per-
fecte inough to his desire, but he woulde giue you the full plott
that shoulde laye out the whole matter.

He denies this, however. Flaskett himself is only asked
whether, having seen the play acted, he proposed improve-
ments and prepared a fuller plot to guide the necessary revision. And this also he denied. They were, of course, bound
to deny it all, because to admit it would be evidence of a
conspiracy to produce the play. As for revision after the
original play was licensed, this would involve them in
difficulties with the Master of the Revels. But we may
reasonably assume, on the whole, that Chapman did, in fact,
plan and write the play of his own accord. Early in the
process, possibly after drawing up his complete plot and
finishing one act of the play, he took his wares to market and
offered it to Woodford. Woodford agreed to accept it when
finished, and probably paid something on account, a procedure that we frequently find in Henslowe's transactions
with dramatists. Woodford was surely reporting mere
current gossip about Flaskett's collaboration in the play.
Flaskett may have encouraged such talk. He may even have
been consulted by Chapman on points of detail. And he
was bound to be very knowing about it all when the play

was discussed among the spectators. Woodford, and the town at large, had indeed a variety of rumours to choose from. One commentator put forward a particularly outrageous theory, which rivals in improbability the wildest guesses of some modern Elizabethan scholarship, and which Woodford duly reports, as an industrious scholar under examination. Its author

did verily perswade himself that Doctor Milward & Chapman were confederate in the Plott of makinge the...Play.

I need hardly say that this was the contribution of that great disintegrator, the incorrigible John Howe, who therein once again recalls Falstaff's genial unconscionableness.

Thus conceived and written, the play was sold to Woodford for twenty marks. The price is a good deal higher than the ordinary market rate for a play in 1603. Chapman, it is true, commanded higher prices from Henslowe than other dramatists. In 1599 he seems to have received from Henslowe for his *All Fools* £8. 10s. 0d., whereas Heywood had £5 in the same year for a play. In 1603 Heywood was paid only £6 for his masterpiece, *A Woman Killed with Kindness*, as compared with Chapman's £13. 6s. 8d. *The Old Joiner of Aldgate* had, of course, found its proper home, and was bound to be a success in the Paul's house, in the very heart of the Stationers' quarter, and in close proximity to the dwellings of the characters of the play. Chapman sold most of his plays, at this stage in his career, to the Children of the Chapel at the Blackfriars theatre. But clearly there were special reasons for dealing in this case with the Children of Paul's.

A very interesting point arises now. In the ordinary course of events, it would be Woodford's next business to get the play licensed by the Master of the Revels, Edmond Tilney, before he could proceed to production on the stage. But in his Answer Woodford stated that he

bought one playe booke of...George Chapman beinge Lycencede

by the Mr of...the quenes maiestyes Revels he not knowinge that yt touchede any person lyvinge.

It is difficult to interpret this otherwise than as meaning that when he bought the play he bought it ready licensed, that Chapman, in fact, saw to the licensing of his play. And it is understandable that this should be a part of Woodford's bargain, when there was a risk that the subject of the play would disqualify it for licence. Indeed, we may well wonder how far this was a practice common among free-lance dramatists in their dealings with the companies. Incidentally, the price paid for *The Old Joiner of Aldgate* would, in this event, include the Revels fee, then seven shillings, not a great matter. Woodford's deposition, it is true, might be read to mean that the licensing of the play came between the time of purchase and the time of acting of the play, but the syntax must be forced to yield this sense.

The play then went forward to rehearsal and production by the Children of Paul's. It seems clear that Woodford was closely associated with this company of actors at this time. Certainly he did not re-sell his play to Edward Peers, the Master of the Children, and thus conclude a mere middle-man's transaction. Peers, we may remember, in his Answer dissociated himself from all financial dealings in plays. His sole concern was with the education and instruction of the Children, so that his function ran parallel with that of the famous Richard Mulcaster, then Master of the Grammar School of Paul's. He repeats the same denial in his examination. Thomas Woodford was alone concerned in the purchase of the play. It appears from Woodford's deposition that he was equally concerned in its production:

he did buy a Stage Play of George Chapman...& paied for the same twentie marks which Play was called the Old Joyner of Algate & was plaied at some severall tymes the last Hillary terme by the Children of Powles by this defendants meanes & appoint-ment but before the plaieng therof the same was licensed to be plaied by the Master of the Revells And further...he hath the

booke itself without alteringe of it to this defendants knowledge
since the last of ffebruary last.

It was then Woodford who was responsible for the play
being acted by the Children. And it is he who remains in
possession of the play-book. It is certain that Woodford was
not merely the financier of a company, like Henslowe, but
that he was the manager and, in a measure, the proprietor
of the Children of Paul's, doubtless by negotiation with Peers
and in partnership with him. Presumably Peers, as Master,
would see to the general maintenance and welfare of the
Children, and would also train and rehearse them for acting.
Woodford would control the finance and the policy of the
company and the theatre, though Peers would be responsible
in all things directly to the Cathedral authorities, whose
connection with the Children, though apparently a real
subsisting connection, probably amounted to little more than
that of their landlord in respect of the singing school in
which they performed their plays, and in other respects was
very ill defined and is now quite obscure. It was Peers also,
we may note, who received payment for performances at
Court by the Children, from 1601 to 1605/6. We must therefore add Woodford to our list of theatrical managers at this
period, and modify accordingly the history of the Children of
Paul's and the biography of this nephew of the poet Thomas
Lodge, who has hitherto been known only through his later
venture in the Whitefriars theatre in 1608, in partnership
with Drayton, Woodford's interest as lessee apparently con-
tinuing until 1621. Presumably his experience at Paul's encouraged him to this second venture. I gather that Woodford's connection with Paul's was severed when Edward
Kirkham joined Peers as 'one of the Masteres of the Children
of Pawles', and took his place, in the winter of 1605/6.

§ v. THE PLAY RECONSTRUCTED

And now to the play itself. I do not know of anything more tantalizing than to read Woodford's deposition, and to hear him answering questions by recommending the Court, for further information, to consult the play-book, Woodford's property. It is indeed suggested that the play-book is available, and it seems possible that it was actually an exhibit in the case. If so, it is lamentable to think that the file of the case might well have contained Chapman's autograph play in full, licensed and prepared for the stage. For elsewhere I have found, in two similar cases in Star Chamber, the copies of more elementary plays attached to the other documents. We were evidently within an ace of having had preserved for us a priceless possession.

In its absence, we must venture upon some attempt to reconstruct the play, which is bound to be highly conjectural. Our starting-point is, of course, our knowledge of the events of the case, together with the date when the play was begun and finished by Chapman. It was begun before Christmas 1602 and was already well under way when Woodford bought it at that time. It was finished soon after Christmas and delivered to Woodford, to be acted during January and February 1603. And Chapman never had it back to be corrected or revised, as he tells us himself. We are therefore clear that the play could not take the action beyond events up to Christmas 1602. The last notable event in the story had been Milward's successful appeal in the Court of Delegates against the decision of the Court of Arches. And doubtless public interest was revived in the story by the approaching re-trial in the same Court, which duly took place in Hilary Term, 1603. When Chapman set to work on his play, therefore, in December 1602, as things then stood the story ended with the defeat of Flaskett and the triumph of Milward. So much for the end.

Where did Chapman begin his story? He was bound to

set forth the preliminary situation out of which the subsequent imbroglio developed. And, in fact, one of the characters of the play is Mrs Glasbie, 'a woman that sold glasses', universally recognized as representing Margaret Sharles, Agnes' aunt, who sold glassware among other things in her shop, the Harrow in Newgate Market.

So it is reasonably clear that the play would have opened at the Harrow, with Mrs Sharles in her shop, probably gossiping with a neighbour or two. The three Howes, father, mother and daughter, might join her, and in the course of the scene Mrs Sharles would announce her intention of making Agnes her heiress. Elizabeth Abbott, Margaret's house-servant, who is needed later on in the Pursuivants scene, would have her part here also. A subsequent scene might take us to a tavern, with comments on Agnes' fortune. I think I see Jones there, and certainly Field, and John Howe joining them and being royally treated for a start. Next would come Flaskett separately, probably at the Howes' house in St Gregory's, in converse with Mrs Howe and Agnes, in the absence of Howe. The first act would thus show us the two opposing parties, Field encouraged by Howe, and Flaskett by Mrs Howe and Agnes, as symmetrical a situation as the heart of a dramatist could desire.

The exposition thus completed, and the preliminary situation thus created, complication would speedily be brought about, in accordance with the title, by which we must not be misled. The Old Joiner of Aldgate is not a carpenter; he is a barber. He is a joiner only in the way of matrimony. And he is 'old' only in the sense of being practised or inveterate or excellent in his quality. The second act, I imagine, would dispose at once of Mrs Sharles, whose death added urgency to the situation. And we should soon see Howe bargaining with Jones, Field and with other suitors, particularly the gentlemanly Humphrey of the Court, introduced one after another, and probably raising his price with each new aspirant, in a strongly 'bull' market. The action would sway probably from the Harrow, with the Howes installed there, to taverns. Here also, I suppose, would be placed the famous trip to Lambeth, shown probably in the Boar's Head Tavern in Old Fish Street on the return of the party.

The third act might open with the betrothal scene of Agnes and Flaskett at the Oswalds' house. Later in the act would follow the great Pursuivants scene at the Harrow, with Elizabeth Abbott bringing beer and alarm to the family party, and ending in the betrothal of Agnes under duress to Field. To complete the comic effect of this scene, and to show Howe turning the tables upon his adversary Jones, a previous scene should show Jones setting his pursuivant on with his warrant against Howe. And here also, in this act, would be the place for a scene in which Humphrey of the Court would be assured by Howe that Agnes was his and his alone, on payment of something on account. And so we should arrive at the height of the complication.

So far we have provided for most of the characters who stand on record, Mrs Glasbie for Margaret Sharles, Snipper Snapper for Howe, Ursula for Agnes, Tresacres for Field, Touchbox for Flaskett, and Umphrevile for Humphrey Rogers. Mrs Howe is not mentioned, but she is clearly indispensable. There remain a French Doctor, and Spitter Spatter. As Snipper Snapper represents a barber, one would expect Spitter Spatter to be a painter. But possibly he was Snipper Snapper's servant, wielding the barber's brush as his master wielded the scissors and razor. I have little doubt that he represented Oswald in a changed capacity, as a sort of parasite to Snipper Snapper. It might perhaps be well to avoid offending the Stationers' Company by making a mere mock of even the least of their freemen. As for the French Doctor, there can be no manner of question but that Milward came on the stage, a pompous Dr Caius, speaking broken French, in this grotesque disguise. How Chapman and Woodford and the actors must have chuckled at Milward's dilemma,

when he came to read the play in the attempt to prove that
he was involved in it! Either he had to let the play go scot-
free, or he had to suffer shipwreck of his dignity in recognizing himself and admitting that this monstrous cap fitted.

The fourth act would very reasonably show us Snipper
Snapper, overwhelmed by suitors, seeking counsel in his
difficulties of this French Doctor, quite possibly followed by
Mrs Howe on a similar errand in support of Flaskett. Thereafter should come complaints from various suitors that
Snipper Snapper was fobbing them off, and a lively scene
might be made of one after another bursting in upon him,
Snipper Snapper hard put to it to get rid of one before the
next came, but still prodigal of assurances and receptive to
donations. We should then see the French Doctor laying his
plots with Mrs Howe and Brampton. Thus the *dénouement*
would be prepared in this act.

The fifth act would bring matters to a head, showing
several suitors revealing to each other that Snipper Snapper
had made promises to all of them, and comparing notes.
Tresacres and Touchbox would proclaim their intention to
proceed to law to enforce their rights. I should have been
sorely tempted to place this scene in front of Christ Church,
and to have begun it with Jones posting up his caveat
against all other suitors of Agnes, making this as it were the
match set to the explosion of Howe's devices. And in the
very height of the argument the French Doctor and Agnes
would enter and announce their marriage, dashing so many
and such incompatible hopes to the ground, including
Snipper Snapper's hopes of further profit. I think I can even
find the right line upon which the play should end, placed
in the mouth of Snipper Snapper, addressed to the unfortunate Tresacres, and adapted from Falstaff in a similarly
disastrous moment of ruin:

Master Tresacres, I owe you five hundred pounds.

The action could hardly take the story further. Chapman

would have to be careful to keep off such dangerous matter
as any parody of proceedings at law, in the Prerogative Court
concerning the estate and the Doctors, or in the Court of
Arches concerning the contracts of marriage. Nor could such
matters well be made amenable to dramatic representation.
So also he was bound to disguise Dr Milward somewhat
heavily, for to caricature the Church was a risky jest. Milward
told Woodford that the play 'directly concerned his cause
& his wives in the Ecclesiasticall Courtes'. But we have seen
how awkward it was for him to assert that the French Doctor
was Dr Milward, even if he had been unmoved by the threat
of a derisive prologue as the actors' revenge for prohibition
of their play on representations by Milward. Chapman
knew his business. And, in any case, the presentable dramatic
part of the story ended with the marriage, which yielded an
excellent catastrophe and left things as they actually were
at the time when the play was written and acted.

This reconstruction of the play depends mainly on a merely
individual notion of how the story as we have it could lend
itself to the form of a five-act comedy. We are given some
of the principal characters to help us. And we may be quite
certain that no dramatist worth his salt would have missed
certain opportunities of using ready-made drama, such as
the Pursuivants scene, or the betrothal scene of Flaskett, or
the irony of Milward's response to Howe's appeal for counsel.
We may be certain also that if Spitter Spatter represented
Oswald he would be 'drunken Oswald' and a source of
mirth. Snipper Snapper-Howe I see as a minor Falstaff, a
humorist as well as an unscrupulous and greedy opportun-
ist. The French Doctor must have been extraordinarily funny
to those in the know, and was probably presented by the
actor who played the part with some smack of Milward's
personality, despite the disguise. It is difficult to say what
impression of Flaskett was conveyed in the play, except that
the portrait seems to have been something of a caricature,
for it is definitely suggested that Flaskett was hurt by the

figure he was made to cut on the stage, on hearing reports of it. The name itself is, of course, a pun, Touchbox being a synonym for flask as a receptacle for powder, just as Tres-acres is a punning version of Field, and Mrs Glasbie's name commemorates Mrs Sharles' trade.

The Old Joiner of Aldgate was acted, according to several concurrent accounts, on 28 February 1603. But it is also stated more than once that it was acted on the very day on which sentence was given in the Court of Delegates, on 20 February. Peers deposes that it was only acted once. But Peers was capable of anything, I fancy. Others aver that it was acted all through the Hilary Term. And Woodford tells us how it was inhibited for a time and then resumed. This is most likely, on the evidence. Moreover, the cost of the play had to be met, and it would certainly run for more than one performance. It was probably a profitable investment, in fact.

We have on record the impressions of certain spectators. Agnes Shaw never went. Nor did Dr Milward. So we miss their views. Edward Brampton saw the play. And Flaskett and Howe went together to see it. Howe tells us that Flaskett and he sat side by side through one performance, and he had no real doubt about the significance of the characters and the action:

there was a stage Play plaied by the children of Powles concerning a barber & others & this defendant thinketh that the same Play was meant by this defendant & his daughter & Mris Sharles John fflaskett & others, att which Play he did once sitt together with fflaskett & sawe the same, being unawares vnto him brought to sitt by fflaskett to see the Play And further he hath heard manie say that the Play was made of this defendant & his daughter & also of others.

The interrogatory makes it plain that it was while they were actually at the play that he heard such comments around him. Flaskett admits that he was there, and is our only authority for Spitter Spatter and the French Doctor, though there is other authority for a Doctor. And Flaskett goes on to give his impression of the play:

he was at the first offended with the Play because it was told this defendant that he was meant by the name of Tuchboxe in the Play and afterwards this defendant sawe the same & then took the same to be but a iest perswading himself that he was not meant thereby but that the same was onely a meere Toye which had idle applications of names according to the Inventors disposicion therof.

Evidently Chapman had modified Flaskett in his stage portrait enough to leave room for some small hesitancy in identification. When Flaskett thus explained to the Court of Star Chamber how he comforted himself as he saw upon the stage the very events of his own life unrolled in the form of a farcical comedy, he had some reason for self-complacency. He had in the interval got his judgment in the Court of Delegates, and things were still going his way, in May 1603. He could still flatter himself into security. But John Howe, whom he took to the theatre, or with whom he was taken, for the fun of watching his surprise and indignation at his reflection in Snipper Snapper the Barber, was of sturdier stuff and turned no blind eye towards the unpalatable truth. When Woodford talked to Howe about the play, Howe's comment was plainly humorous:

he had no reason to take it to himself for that Kings had been presented on the stage & therefore Barbers might.

The milk was spilt, Flaskett's cake was dough, Milward had Agnes with what was left of her estate. But Howe had feathered his nest, and there was no doubt about that. He might well be philosophical about taking his place for a while on the London stage and hobnobbing there, even in a pillory, with the nobility and gentry and royalty. After all, he had had the honour of sitting for his portrait to a very great artist. And we are left with a very uncomfortable problem.

Whom else, besides Kings and Barbers, did the Elizabethan and Jacobean stage present? Here is a specific and

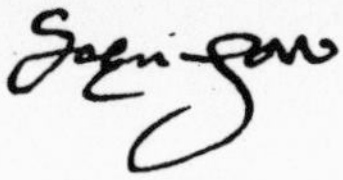

PLATE I

JOHN HOW

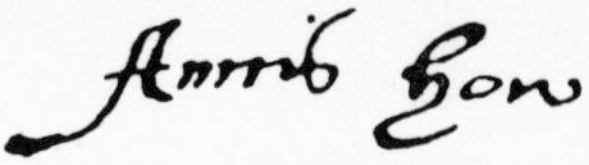

ANNIS (AGNES) HOW

JOHN FLASKETT

JOHN MYLLWARD

THOMAS WOODFORD

EDWARD PEERS

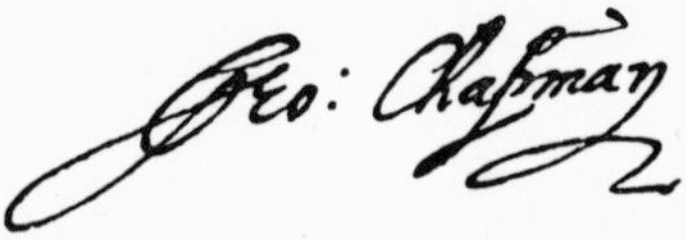

GEORGE CHAPMAN

A. M(OUNDS)
ANNE ELSDON

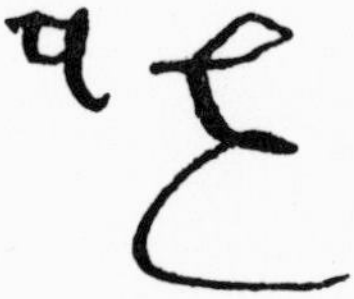

A. H.
AARON HOLLAND

THOMAS DEKKER

A PAGE OF SIGNATURES

certain instance of the topical drama, of the stage as news-paper in effect, in 1603, to set alongside *Keep the Widow Waking* in 1623. Had these plays alone survived, in print, instead of these records of actual events which begot them, who would have even suspected the stories that lay behind them, except for the murder part of the story of Dekker's play?

Indeed, who knows what fanciful exegesis might not have been applied to Chapman's play, with such a suggestive story? What hard heart would not receive it for an allegory of Queen Elizabeth with her many suitors at auction for her favour? Would not the French Doctor suitably cloak the Duke of Alençon? Such ingenuities, even in the despite of dates, might well have flown free. But for once the play is lost, and the facts are found. And they are instructive.

We know that Ben Jonson brought Inigo Jones and Nathaniel Butter on the stage. But who knows what else of real life the comedies of Jonson or Middleton conceal in the mask of a stage reflection? It is well to bear in mind Chapman's evasions in Star Chamber concerning the topical significance of *The Old Joiner of Aldgate*, when we read the frequent and reiterated protestations of Elizabethan drama-tists, in prologues to plays accused of similar purposes. It may be that the topical bases of many a play are indeed of such humble stuff as this, and are not to be sought by that more dangerous inquisition which affirms, in Ben Jonson's words,

what Mirror of Magistrates is meant by the justice, what great lady by the pigwoman, what concealed statesman by the seller of mouse-traps.

If Snipper Snapper was in reality a barber, may not many pigwomen or sellers of mouse-traps be in fact pigwomen and sellers of mouse-traps?

(ii) *Keep the Widow Waking*

by Dekker, Rowley, Ford
and Webster

§ i. THE OLD BAILEY & STAR CHAMBER

At the Gaol Delivery from Newgate on 3 September 1624 there came forth for trial at the Old Bailey Tobias Audley for felony, and Nathaniel Tindall for murder. Audley was put back on remand, and lingered on in gaol till he died. Tindall was found guilty and was executed. Meanwhile the stage of the Red Bull theatre in Clerkenwell had seized upon them, making a jest of the one, and melodrama of the other, in frequent performances of what seems to have been a successful play in which both figured, written by four of the most famous dramatists of the time. There was, perhaps, more true mercy in the Courts of Justice.

The play is generally referred to in our sources of information as *Keep the Widow Waking*, though its full title as given by Dekker, one of its authors, in a Star Chamber document, is 'The late Murder in White Chappell, or Keepe the Widow waking'. The joint authors were Dekker, Rowley, Ford and Webster. Sir Henry Herbert's Office Book records the licensing of the play. But no trace of it is to be found anywhere else save in the records of proceedings at law. From them, however, the facts of the matter, and the nature of the play, may be set forth in remarkably full detail. The crimes with which Audley was charged, and the play which made them its theme, became inseparably associated in the resentment of injured parties, and furnished material for a suit in Star Chamber. The records of this suit are admirably complete, lacking only the decree of the Court, whose decisions are almost invariably to be known only from other sources.

And it is happily possible, with the help of interpolations and additions, to trace various stages in the enquiry.

Certain documents contained among the Proceedings are especially interesting. A most unusual document is 'The Answer of Thomas Dekker one of the Defendants', dated 3 February 1625, which I judge to be undeniably autograph. Evidently the dramatist drew up his Answer himself, wrote it out fair, and subsequently had it slightly revised and signed by a lawyer, Nathaniel Finch. It is a most unorthodox form of Answer, and does not contain the usual safeguarding preliminaries. We may ask ourselves whether Dekker was independent or confident enough to consider such a task to be well within his own powers. Certainly he has his fling at lawyers in his known plays. Or he may simply have been desirous of saving money. But in the end he had to resort to professional skill to amend his private efforts. Among other documents of interest to the historian of the Elizabethan stage, there are signed depositions of Dekker, of Aaron Holland, the owner of the site and theatre, and of Ellis Worth, the principal actor of the company occupying it and performing this play.

The Bill of Information contains the full text of a ballad in two parts narrating one of the two stories out of which the play was made, and giving a popular version of the events which led to the appeal to the Star Chamber. The Bill also enables us to date the death of William Rowley, one of the dramatists concerned. From Dekker's Answer and Deposition we learn a good deal about the genesis and writing of the play, including the part for which he was personally responsible. And some of the evidence, as well as the Bill, bears upon an appeal to the Master of the Revels, to whom Dekker also refers.

The whole story throws light not only upon the workings of the popular stage, but also upon the sordid and unpleasant underworld of London, with its impecunious and blackguardly fortune-hunters battening upon an intemperate old widow of means. With the help of the Star Chamber records, and other sources of information, notably from the Middlesex Sessions, we can complete an account of the story on which the comic part of the play was founded, and learn all we need to know about the murder which furnished its tragic plot.

Incongruous as was the linking together of these two stories into one play, in which no possible dramatic connection could give them any artistic unity, it was evidently sufficient for the dramatist exploiting topical interest that the two wretched criminals involved lay in the same gaol together and were led forth on the same day to stand at the bar of judgment. The coincidence serves only to deepen in our minds the impression of that strange and forbidding heartlessness which the Jacobean age so often reflects in its drama as elsewhere.

§ ii. THE ADVENTURE OF ANNE ELSDON

We may judge from the story of Anne Elsdon and Tobias Audley how far it was fitted for a comic plot. It is essential to have it in some detail if we are to understand the ballad and the information given concerning the play. And it furnishes an admirable commentary upon such a play as Ben Jonson's *The Alchemist*, with its shady crew of dissolute scamps. One of Audley's crew, Holiday, like Subtle, was a 'reputed Coniuror, and teller of fortunes'.

The unfortunate heroine was the widow of John Elsdon or Ellesden, described as a gentleman, whom she had married at St Martin's-in-the-Fields on 21 January 1591, at the age of twenty-nine. She was now sixty-two years of age. And it was in this late autumn of her life that her modest fortune set dangerous toils about her path. A mysterious reference, during the Star Chamber proceedings, to a proposed pleasure-jaunt to Anne's house at Romford, is explained by footprints in the sands of Chancery which lead back to the

days of Henry VIII. Anne's grandmother, Katharine Down-
ham, owned the George Inn at Romford, and her daughter
Isabel brought it as part of her dowry to her husband
John Mounds[1] of the same town, described as a merchant-
man, aged twenty-eight on 15 November 1555. From his
father Richard he inherited some score of acres of land, Bery
Mead, Bery Field, Braybrooke and Gybbs, together with a
horse-mill. He was obviously a substantial Romford citizen.
And the George Inn had been in the family for some sixty
years when his daughter and heiress Anne married Elsdon.
Elsdon was some three or four years younger than his wife,
and was some kind of a clerk or surveyor in Stepney in 1598.
They had an only child, Elizabeth, named after Anne's
sister, married to a highly respectable Londoner, Benjamin
Garfield, of St James, Clerkenwell. Three grandchildren
had died during the last seven years. But one son, Benjamin, survived, though still an infant as yet, destined to
play some small part in dramatic history in due course.
His father doubtless forgot that there were other Bens to
take after when he gave him his own name.

The elder Benjamin, now in his forty-third year, took a
notable interest in the belated adventures of his hitherto
respectable mother-in-law which were to become matters
of lamentable record. He had financial reasons for taking a
hand when those adventures involved the dissipation of his
wife's expectations. And he had already shown his intoler-
ance of all forms of Bohemianism. In consequence of his
zeal, indeed, he had even come to know his way about Star
Chamber, some five years before these events. For in his
capacity as Keeper, Beadle, or Master of Bridewell, that
famous House of Correction, he had imprisoned a certain
Alice Wilton, who lived in Artillery Lane, 'a place of resort

---

[1] Anne's maiden name, 'Anna Mumes', as given in the printed
Register of Marriages of St Martin's-in-the-Fields, is apparently a mis-
reading of 'Anna Munds', a mistake easy to make in transcribing from
Elizabethan handwriting.

and a receptacle of dishonest and disordered persons'. He had, moreover, supplied her, we are told, with 'a Red Wastcoat stripped,[1] with red silk Laces', a picturesque phrase of the time for a whipping, as a promoter of incontinence. Alice, and an unforeseen husband whom she produced, retorted in Star Chamber, with a charge of libel, but I am pretty sure that Garfield was in no danger of losing the case. He was, at any rate, by nature and by his office, as well as by his private interests, well qualified to disapprove of such goings on as those which attracted, and finally overwhelmed, his mother-in-law.

Mrs Elsdon lived in her own house in West Smithfield, not far from her daughter and son-in-law, and not far from the Red Bull theatre in St John Street, Clerkenwell. But she also had familiar acquaintance of a baser sort in her declining years. One of these was a young man, Tobias Audley, who is described in the Bill of Information to the King as 'of Wood streete in your Cittye of London, a keeper of a Tobacco shoppe and a most notorious Lewd person and of noe worth of Creditt'. The King disapproved heartily of tobacco, and presumably of its retail vendors. And inability to obtain credit has always been a handicap, not least in the highly complicated economic world of Jacobean London; such a reputation rendered a man liable to grave suspicion. However this might be, Audley was a suitor in the way of marriage to the old widow whose company he frequented. It is true that he was a widower himself, but in no other respect was he a suitable match. I gather that he was about twenty-five years of age, if one may strike a medium between defence and prosecution evidence. His motive was clear enough. Mrs Elsdon's property was valued by a witness who had doubtless gone into the question with some care, her son-in-law Garfield, at £90 a year in lands with personal estate to the value of £1000. Local gossip credited her with an estate of £6000 in all. This was no mean fortune.

It is fairly clear that Anne had proclivities which made her

[1] I.e. *striped*.

easy of approach, and that her troubles arose in the first instance from visits to taverns in disreputable company before her last disastrous venture upon conviviality. Audley, a seller of tobacco and spirits, was a queer companion for her even in the democratic society of the City. It is agreed on all hands that he was her suitor. Differences of opinion begin with the question of her reception of his suit. The defence claims that she was inclined to accept his suit, and finally did marry him by her own consent, given after a drinking party at the Greyhound Tavern in Blackfriars, kept by Robert Taylor. The prosecution urges that she refused to consider the suit of 'this beggerlie boy', sought escape from his assiduities, and only consented to meet him in the tavern 'to drink a quart of wyne...for a farewell...in hope to be Rydde and freed from...Audeley and his further daylie solicitacion'.

The whole series of events, indeed, is narrated by defence and prosecution in totally different lights. The narrative is further complicated by a good deal of confusion and conflict of evidence of fact, and the Information is singularly inaccurate in many respects. Here we must seek to disentangle the probable truth, and tell the story underlying the play of *Keep the Widow Waking*, to the best of our judgment, as a consistent whole.

About eight o'clock on the evening of Wednesday, 21 July 1624, Anne Elsdon, accompanied by her friend Martha Jackson, aged forty-eight, wife of a shoemaker, went with Audley on his invitation to the Greyhound Tavern. They were shown into a private room, and found there awaiting them a motley company which included two disreputable ministers of religion, Nicholas Cartmell and Francis Holiday, and two women of easy virtue, Mary Spenser of Charterhouse Lane, of the junior branch of her profession, and her 'Nurse', as she calls her, Margery Terry. Anne and Martha were plied generously with drink, and it was hoped that Anne would declare before witnesses that she would accept Audley as her husband and so contract herself to him. All present were in the plot and were to profit from the resulting marriage, Audley having promised sums varying from £100 to Holiday to £20 to Terry, and the reversion of his tobacco shop to Edmond Hide, his assistant or servant. It appears that the two scandalous old men, Holiday and Cartmell, and the bawd Terry were the prime movers who devised the scheme. Holiday's 'sonne' Audley, as he called him, was to sue Anne persistently by ordinary means, and when this failed or hung fire, to have recourse to more sinister practices.

Both Anne and Martha drank to excess at the Greyhound. Martha was relegated to the kitchen, where she spent an unhappy night. Taylor shut up his house, a bed or pallet was set up for Anne, and the whole party stayed there all night. On the following morning, Thursday, Martha went home, but Anne was taken by Audley, Cartmell, and Terry across the river to Lambeth and into St George's Fields, and had more drink there. Returning to London, they brought her to another tavern, the Nag's Head in Cheapside, kept by Francis Wise. There the same company gathered together again, and the unfortunate woman was kept there three days and nights in a constant state of drunkenness. She was given wine in quantities, together with such 'hot waters' or spirits as *aqua vite, rosa solis,* and *humm.* (The Court evinced unusual interest in *humm,* but obtained no answer to their curious inquiries concerning 'the signification of *humm*'.)[1] The wife of Hide, one of the crew, confessed 'with weeping teares that after...An Ellesden came to the...Nags Head tauerne she was very sicke and sencles and yet the defendants did powre downe such vialls of hot waters downe her throate that she thought was able to kill a horse'.[2] The bawd Terry indeed feared she would die, and so protested to Audley, who replied unfeelingly, 'lett her bee hangde, Ile haue her

---

[1] The philological evidence suggests that it was, like the German 'Hummel-Wasser', from which it was possibly derived, a strong decoction of mead.

[2] *Deposition of John Davis* 'of the parish of St. Olaue in the Borough of Southwarke, dier, aged 42', a rival suitor, I fancy.

goods and lett them take her lands'. Anne still held out in
spite of this, however, and drugs were sent for and used by
Cartmell, who is described by one John Snowe who turned
King's evidence as 'faine to raise some meane maintenance
by a supposed skill in phisicke, and some other discredited
courses'.

Some form of contract of marriage was gone through on
this first evening at the Nag's Head, which consisted of Cartmell placing Anne's hand in Audley's before witnesses. The
key of Anne's house, furthermore, was taken from her pocket,
and Audley and Wise went there and brought back about
£20, limiting their depredations for the moment to meet
present necessities, including the cost of a marriage licence.
The licence was obtained next day, Friday, 23 July, from the
Chancellor of the Bishop of London's office, with the help
of a Proctor of their acquaintance, William Durham. Apparently young Hide was sent for it, and Audley paid the fee.
The record remains in the *Vicar-General's Papers*, vol. 1, at
Somerset House, and reads as follows, with the abbreviations
filled in:

Licentia	vicesimo tertio die mensis Julii Anno domini
matrimonii	1624 emanavit licentia Rectori vicario seu Curato
inter	ecclesie parochialis Sancti Bartholomei magni
Audley et	London ad solemnizandum matrimonium inter
Elsnor	Tobiam Audley Stiller et Anne Elsnor parochio
	Sancti Bartholomei magni London viduam re-
	lictam (*blank*) Elsnor defuncti in unica bannorum
	edicione vt moris est Ac ita vt nullum inde
	generetur preiudicium etc.

The licence thus granted permitted the marriage to be
celebrated by any of the clergy of St Bartholomew's the
Great at that church, without preliminary publication of
banns. Difficulties arose. Cartmell at first refused to officiate
in the tavern. Audley saw Durham again and asked for a
dispensation for the place. This being impossible, he decided
to marry her first and seek a dispensation afterwards, on the

ground that Anne had refused to go to church, having no fitting clothes and being unwell. On his return, about noon on the 23rd, Cartmell performed a ceremony of marriage. We need not be surprised that my search of the Parish Registers for a record of the marriage was fruitless, though even irregular marriages were sometimes registered subsequently in the Church Books. Anne was evidently in a state of alcoholic coma. Mary Spenser related, on examination before Justice Ducket, that she found Anne sitting in a chair like a sick person. When Cartmell read the words asking her if she would have Audley to husband, as she was unable to speak, Spenser 'did take her by the Chin and strike her teeth together to cause her to answer, which she not doing...Cartmell reiterated the words but had not any answer from...An Elesden'. Snowe, after the ceremony, 'said hee would goe in, and bidd God give her ioy, and when hee came in, hee found her sitting in a chaire, leaning her bodie all on one side, and driveling, and this deponent speaking somewhat lowd vnto her, and shaking her, and bidding God give her ioy, shee was vnable to speake vnto him againe'. Thereafter what had taken place at the Blackfriars tavern was repeated; a bed was set up for Anne, Audley put off his clothes, came to the company and cried 'all was his nowe', and 'then went into the roome where...Anne so lay distempered, and went to bedd to her'.

I have little doubt that this is the true story, and that the pictures of love and merriment on both sides, drawn by Audley, Holiday, Ward, and two of the tavern-keepers, Hopkins and Wise, represent some hard lying and revolting heartlessness, which later events emphasize.

The day of the marriage was spent by the company in drunken revelry in the Nag's Head, keeping open house for their friends and relations at Anne's expense. The bill in the end amounted to between £20 and £25. Next morning, Saturday, Anne protested that she was not Audley's wife, and told Snowe tragically 'that shee was married to no one butt to her grave'. The conspirators, secure in their success, now had nothing but taunts for her. She was shown the marriage licence, jeered at as 'old hag' and 'old jade', and when the harlot Mary Spenser suggested to Audley that he might 'make much of her, and soe stop her exclamacions', Audley replied 'that hee had as leive goe to bedd to an old Sowe'. The only remedy to Anne's griefs that was applied was strong drink, and she was soon drunk again.

But trouble now began. Audley believed himself to be master of her fortune, and he was probably on his way to Anne's house when Garfield fired his first shot. Audley was arrested at his suit, but was bailed by the help of his brother John, and apparently this charge dropped. So Audley was able to spend the Saturday night rifling Anne's house, from which he brought away £120 in gold, £20 in rings and plate, and various deeds and bonds. The disintegration of her estate was well under way. What went on in the Nag's Head on Saturday and Sunday may be imagined from the contents of the play, and from evidence of next-door neighbours. Sara Pickes, a goldsmith's wife, heard 'a woman crying out in the said Roome I will go home, I will go home...making great moane that she was deteyned there against her will diuerse persons in the said roome telling her that she should not go'. Frances Streete, the young wife of a Broad Street hosier, heard her 'bewaile and bemone her misfortune saying o lord o lord I am vndone: wherunto some person then presente made answeare...wee willbe merry and haue our coach and six horses and so goe see your howse att Rumford'.

Meanwhile Anne's daughter and her husband Garfield were seeking for the vanished widow, and Robert Boulton, a West Smithfield stationer, who owed Anne £20, and bought his bond of Audley for £5 as his share of the spoils, put them off the scent by directing them to Romford. The desire to keep Anne concealed led to a further change of haunt. A visit of suspicious churchwardens to the Nag's

Head on Sunday morning hastened the move. The unfortunate victim was taken to the Bell Tavern in Wood
Street, suspected of being a disorderly house, where Audley
lodged, on Sunday evening the 25th. There, according to
the tavern-keeper, Thomas Hopkins, 'thay boath lay in
bedd together...all that night and spent the next day in
meryment, and at night about Tenn of the Clocke thay were
lighted home to the house of ...Anne by one of...(Hopkins's) servaunts'.

Thus Anne was returned to her devastated house on
Monday night, and it may be gathered that Audley left her
there. He had been unable to obtain from her legal assign-
ments of her lands, but was alarmed at the threats of Mrs Garfield to break open Anne's house in search of her. Anne was
in no better case than her house, and it is said that she lay ill
or stupid and senseless 'and in a manner speecheles' for nine
or ten days after. It is difficult to be sure what Audley had
gained. The prosecution alleged that he had carried off £3000
worth of documents, and doubtless Anne's securities were
dealt in to some extent. He had taken £120 in cash, and a
good deal of plate. But the tavern expenses for the five days'
revels were heavy, £50 in all. He was also committed to
share out over £300 to the conspirators, and doubtless their
demands were the first to be satisfied. Garfield deposed that
Audley in the space of five weeks had wasted the whole of
Anne's personal estate, £1000, and was trying to borrow
money.

It remains to trace the aftermath of these proceedings,
leaving for the moment the question of the play and ballad
which reflected them. Dissensions among the thieves broke
out early. Mary Spenser quarrelled with Cartmell over her
share, and got Snowe to write for her a most incriminating
letter to him, threatening to go to Garfield and 'hang them
all'. Cartmell and Holiday sought to make their peace with
Garfield, suggesting payment for their offer to deny the
marriage, 'and ye said Cartmell shold goe into Ireland & soe

noe priest noe marriage to be proued', to which Garfield
replied offering to present them with sixpence to buy a
halter for themselves.[1] On 8 August Audley was involved
in a brawl at Garfield's house, to which Anne had been taken.
Probably Audley insisted on seeing his 'wife' and pressed his
marital claims, especially financial. His visit had violent con-
clusions, and gave Garfield good grounds for setting the law
in motion against Audley and also against his companions.

Proceedings now began at the Middlesex Sessions. On
9 August Audley, described for once at least as 'generosus',
appeared before Justice Williamson, with five friends, including Edmond Ward, one of the defendants, here described as of the Inner Temple, Gentleman,[2] to give recognizances in £20 each for Audley's appearance at the next
Sessions, 'and in the meane time to keep the peace against our
soveraigne Lord the king & all his people especially against
one Mr Garfeild'. On 25 August Robert Butcher, a tailor,
was bound to appear at the next Sessions, 'beeing bound to
doe his best endeavor to produce Mary Spenser and Mar-
garett Terry which hee hath not done therfor to Answer
such matters on his Majesties behalfe as shall be objected
against him by Mr Garfeild'. The words added, 'ven et exor
Rog Horton', show that Justice Horton acquitted him on
his appearance. Terry evidently disappeared for a time, but
Spenser was soon in custody. Audley surrendered to his
recognizances and was lodged in 'the newe prison'.[3]

On 1 September Audley and Spenser both appeared at the
Sessions of Peace, at Hicks Hall in John Street, and were
committed to gaol, to be brought up again before the Justices
of Peace. Spenser was bailed on 4 September, her sureties
being John May of St Giles'-in-the-Fields, gentleman, and

---

[1] *Deposition of Frances Fuller*, 'wiefe of Tho: Fuller of Steben in the
Countie of Essex clerke aged 32'. Fuller was the messenger to Garfield.

[2] But Snowe describes him as 'held to bee a Common Taverne fol-
lower, and to live in a kind of roaring fashion, without credit or esteeme'.

[3] Sessions Rolls 630/252, 'A Calendar for the newe prison the ferste
of September 1624'.

Butcher. Audley next appears on 3 September on the Gaol Delivery from Newgate, at the Old Bailey, on the charge of assault. A True Bill was returned by the Grand Jury, which runs as follows:

po se

Juratores pro dno Rege super sacrm suum presentant qd Tobias Audley nuper de Clarkenwell in Com Midd yom octavo die Augusti Anno Regni dni nri Jacobi dei gra Anglie ffrancie et Hibnie Regis fidei defensr &c vicesimo scdo et Scotie lviij vi et Armis &c apud Clarkenwell pd in Com pd in et super quandam Annam Elsdon in pace dei et dci dni Regis nunc adtunc et ibm existen insult fecit Et ipsam Annam Elsdon adtunc et ibm verber-avit et vulneravit et maletractavit Ita qd de vita eius desperabatur et alia enorma eidem Anne Elsdon adtunc et ibm intulit ad graue dampnum ipius Anne Et contra pacem dci dni Regis nunc Coronam et dignitat suas

Beniamin Garfeild pros
Katerin Jorden   Will Dugdale   Anne Baylie

Audley is here accused by Garfield of an aggravated assault and other enormities on Anne, to the endangering of her life, on 8 August in Clerkenwell, to which charge he pleaded not guilty (*posuit se* non culpabilem). When he came to trial on this charge in the course of the Sessions, before Justice Daniell, he was acquitted of the felony alleged. The entry is as follows:

ven et exor

Tobias Audley de poch sci Sepulchri Lond Chirurgion pro suss felon   Wm Daniell

The versatile Audley, gentleman, tobacconist, seller of potent spirits, has here assumed the trade and name of a surgeon.

At the General Sessions at Westminster on 30 September Audley was brought up again from Newgate. Both Audley and Spenser were once more remanded. A third culprit, an obscure 'Clerke', Thomas Fuller, whose wife, Frances Fuller, of Stebbing, Essex, gave evidence in the Star Chamber, was also examined, 'being suspected to be A procurer of an vn-lawfull Marryadge betwene Tobias Audley and Ann

Elesden', and was acquitted at a later Session on 8 December, before Justice Longe.

At the Gaol Delivery on 4 October Audley appeared again before Justice Williamson on some alternative charge, and was committed without bail to the next Sessions at the Old Bailey. On 6 December Mary Spenser made her third appearance at the Sessions of the Peace at Hicks Hall. The charge was 'practizing an vnlawfull Marryadge betweene Tobias Audley and Anne Elesden', and she was acquitted by Justice Horton.

Audley appears again in connection with Gaol Deliveries on 8 December, when he was remanded for the carrying out of a previous order, and on 17 January 1624/5, when he was again remanded at the instance of the Lord Mayor of London. The matter had long since passed out of the hands of the Middlesex Justices. Garfield perceived that his charges against his enemies under the Common Law were not effective, one after another charge failing. The whole question had been further complicated by the play and ballad. He therefore took the matter to the Court of Star Chamber, and laid an Information there, which the Attorney-General sponsored. The Bill of Information is dated 26 November. The Answers of Audley and his friends are dated 10 December, and those of the theatre people involved from Dekker's on 3 January to Holland's on 5 February. Terry's Answer is in the nature of a confession, and is dated 31 January. The Interrogatories to the Defendants are dated 4 January, and the depositions of Audley's friends were taken from 13 January to 27 January. The Interrogatories to Prosecution witnesses were drawn up on 25 February, and Snowe was examined on 27 February. But the case dragged on interminably during 1625 and until after July 1626, with new matter and new prosecution witnesses.

In the meantime the principal parties had died. Anne Elsdon was dead before 24 March 1626, as Martha Jackson's evidence shows, and possibly died much earlier. Frances

Fuller's evidence shows that Audley had died before 10 July 1625. And we may assume, from the absence of any deposition by Audley, that he died in Newgate shortly after the last reference to him in the Middlesex records on 19 January 1625. I have failed to find any record of the burial of either. Cartmell also was dead, as an entry in the Parish Register of Guilsborough, of which he was Vicar, records his burial on 9 January 1626. It is likely that the Star Chamber trial died of protraction, and that Garfield's desire for vengeance faded, with the impossibility of recovering the lost goods, and with the death of the principal offender, Audley. It may be added that the Information certainly left many loopholes by its inaccuracies of statement, and by the vagueness of its charges. Garfield himself died on 18 October 1630, at the age of forty-eight, and was buried in St James's, Clerkenwell.

§ iii. THE MURDER IN WHITECHAPEL

The murder which furnished the play with its serious matter may be dealt with more briefly. The records of the Middlesex Sessions give the facts that are important in the eyes of the law. Nathaniel Tindall or Grindall, of Whitechapel, yeoman, murdered Joan Tindall or Grindall on 9 April 1624 in Whitechapel. He came to trial at the Old Bailey at the Gaol Delivery from Newgate, along with Tobias Audley, on Friday, 3 September.[1] The Grand Jury returned a True Bill which I give here as it is written:

Cogn Ss ppe domu vbi ppetrauit murdrum

Midd Juratores pro dno Rege super sacrm suu presentant qd Nathaniel Tindall als Grindall nuper de Whitechappell in Com

---

[1] Gaol Delivery Register, vol. 3, fol. 128b:
Cogn ss
Nathaniel Tindall als Grindall pro murdro Johanne Tindall als Grindall.
The letters *ss* appear again in the margin, with the usual grim flourish and loop, a vivid, if fortuitous, image of the execution thereby recorded.

Midd yom deu pre oculis suis non hens sed instigacone diabolica
motus et seduct nono die Aprilis Anno Regni dni nri Jacobi dei
gra Anglie ffrancie et Hibnie Regis fidei defensr &c vicesimo scdo
et Scotie lvij vi et Armis &c apud Whitechappell pd in Co Pd in
et super quand Johannam Tindall als Grindall adtunc et ibm in
pace dei et dci dni Regis existen felonice voluntar et ex malitia
sua precogitat insult fecit Et qd idem Nathaniel Tindall als
Grindall cu quod Cultello de ferro et Calibe ad valanc vnius denar
quod ipe idem Nathaniel Tindall als Grindall in manu sua dextra
adtunc et ibm huit et tenuit pfat Johanna Tindall als Grindall in
et sup guttur angce the throate ipius Johanne adtunc et ibm
felonice voluntar et ex malitia sua precogitat pcussit angce did
strike dans eid Johanne Tindall als Grindall cu pd Cultello in et
super guttur ipius Johanne vn plagam mortal angce one mortall
wound longitud quatuor polliciu et pfunditat dimid pollicis Et
qd pd Nathaniel Tindall als Grindall cu Cultello pd qd ipe in
manua [*sic*] sua dextra adtunc et ibm huit et tenuit pfat Johanna
in et sup pectus ppe sinistra mamilla angce the lefte dugg ipius
Johanne adtunc et ibm felonice voluntar et ex malitia sua precogitat pupigit angce did stabb dans eid Johanne adtunc et ibm
cu Cultello pd et sup pd pectus ppe dcam sinistram mamilla ipius
Johanne vn mortal vulnus longitud dimid vnius pollicis et pfunditat duor polliciu de quo mortal vulnere in et sup pectus ipius
Johanne ead Johanna adtunc et ibm instant obijt Et sic Juratores
pd dicunt sup sacrm suu qd pd Nathaniel Tindall als Grindall pfat
Johanna Tindall als Grindall pd nono die Aprilis Anno supd modo
et forma pd apud Whitechappell pd in Com felonice voluntar et
ex malitia sua pcogitat interfecit et murdravit Contra pace dci dni
Regis nunc Coron et dignitat suas.

Armigell Seeler Tho. Mathewes Pss.[1]

It appears from this that Tindall assaulted a certain Joan
Tindall with a knife of iron and steel, striking her in the
throat and in the left breast. The second wound was mortal,
and she died instantly. The jury returned a Bill of wilful

---

[1] Sessions Rolls 636/88. Jeaffreson, *Middlesex County Records*, II. 179,
calendars this murder, dating the Bill 17 January 1625 instead of 3 September 1624. The Bill is misplaced among other documents pertaining to the
later date. He also refers to it as a wife-murder, instead of matricide.
The legal documents give no information on this point.

murder. The words above the Bill were written after the trial, and record the judgment. Expanded and translated, they run thus, 'having pleaded guilty, he was sentenced to be hanged near the house where he committed the murder'.

The Rolls occasionally contain records of Coroners' Inquests, but there is no record of an inquest upon Joan Tindall which might have given more detail, possibly even the motive, now lost to our knowledge.

But the unusual quality of the crime led to the production of two ballads, which are recorded in the Stationers' Registers. From these entries we learn that the murdered woman was Tindall's mother. The entries are as follows:

2 Julij 1624. Richard Hodgkins. *The repentance of* NATHANAEL
          TINDALL *that kil(le)d his mother*...   vjd.
16° Septembris John Trundle Richard Hodgkins. Entred for
1624.   their Copie vnder the handes of master Doctor
          WORRALL and master Lownes Warden....*A
          most bloudy vnnaturall and vnmatchable murther
          Comitted in Whitechappell by* NATHANAELL TIN-
          DALL *vpon his owne mother* written by JOHN
          MORGAN....   vjd.[1]

(We shall meet with Hodgkins again in connection with the ballad of *Keep the Widow Waking*.) The story was thus suitable for treatment in a play for the Red Bull. It was notorious enough, and horrible enough, to attract an audience avid of sensations, and to exercise the pen of a Dekker. For Dekker wrote part of *The Late Murder in Whitechapel*, as well as of *Keep the Widow Waking*, and from his reference to his share in it we learn with some additional sense of pain that Tindall was only a youth. The stage, we feel, might have spared him.

The documents give us very little information about the handling of this tragic story in the play. Of the two ballads, the first only is extant, in the Library of the Society of Antiquaries, and it gives no information about the crime. It was 'Printed at London for John Trundle', and bears no date.

[1] Arber, IV. 120, 123.

PLATE II

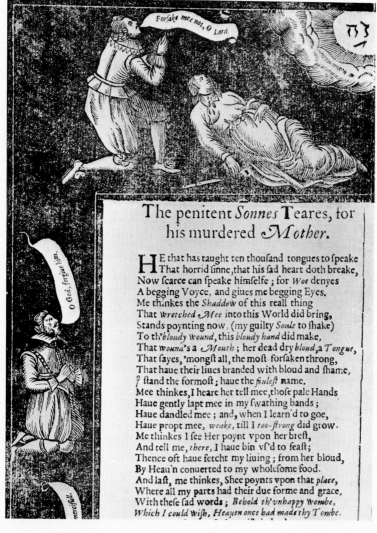

The penitent *Sonnes* Teares, for his murdered *Mother*.

HE that has taught ten thousand tongues to speake
That horrid sinne, that his sad heart doth breake,
Now scarce can speake himselfe ; for *Woe* denyes
A begging Voyce, and giues me begging Eyes.
Me thinkes the *Shaddow* of this reall thing
That *wretched Mee* into this World did bring,
Stands poynting now, (my guilty *Soule* to shake)
To th'*bloudy wound*, this *bloudy hand* did make,
That *wound's* a *Mouth* ; her dead dry *bloud*, a *Tongue*,
That sayes, 'mongst all, the most-forsaken throng,
That haue their liues branded with bloud and shame,
I stand the formost ; haue the *foulest* name.
Mee thinkes, I heare her tell mee, those pale Hands
Haue gently lapt mee in my swathing bands ;
Haue dandled mee ; and, when I learn'd to goe,
Haue propt mee, *weake*, till I *too-strong* did grow.
Me thinkes I see Her poynt vpon her brest,
And tell me, *there*, I haue bin vs'd to feast ;
Thence oft haue fetcht my liuing ; from her bloud,
By Heau'n conuerted to my wholesome food.
And last, me thinkes, Shee poynts vpon that *place*,
Where all my parts had their due forme and grace,
With these sad words ; *Behold th'vnhappy Wombe*,
Which I could wish, Heauen once had made thy Tombe.

THE MURDER BALLAD
From Society of Antiquaries, *Broadsides*, vol. 21, no. 243

The title is *The penitent Sonnes Teares, for his murdered Mother*, and it purports to be written 'By Nathaniel Tyndale, *sicke both in soule and body: a prisoner now in New-gate*'. The text, in heroic couplets, might apply to any repentant murderer, and is printed in the left-hand column. In the right-hand column is another murder-ballad. The sheet has a deep black surround, and several woodcuts illustrating both murders.

The question with which Garfield was concerned is naturally more fully dealt with, and we can reconstruct fairly satisfactorily the version of the story of Anne Elsdon and Tobias Audley that formed the plot of the play of *Keep the Widow Waking*.

§ iv. THE PLAY AT THE RED BULL

The narrative of the events that led Audley and Tindall to their trials in Courts of Justice has been given with reasonable completeness, together with an account of the legal proceedings. We may now turn to their reflection in the world of the stage.

The Bill of Information in the Star Chamber suit against Audley and others, having recited at length the story of the unlawful marriage as it appeared to the prosecution, proceeds further with a statement of events subsequent to this marriage. The complaint is made that Anne Elsdon's estate was shared among the conspirators; that they 'plyed her with seuerall sorts of wyne and stronge waters for many dayes together'; that they did 'watch...Anne Elsden both day and night and kept her from sleepe diuers dayes and nights together'; and finally that they

intending forthwith to make a Iest of merryment of their vnlawfull & wicked accions...thereby to scandalize & disgrace... Anne Elsden & to make her infamous thereby to giue some Collour to the...pretended marriage...Tobias Audeley and the ...other Confederates did most vnlawfully and wickedly practise

resolue and agree to drawe into their practise one William Rowley
now dead   Aron Holland Thomas ffuller clerk Raphe Savadge
(*blank*) deckers, Richard Hodskyns ^ and others being Comon
enterlude players, and contrivors of libellous playes and balletts
which should contriue & make a play and balletts of the. . .pre-
tended marriage. . ., and the ryfeling and getting of. . .Anne
Elsden's estate. . ., According to which. . .wicked & vnlawfull
practise & resolucion. . .Tobias Audley and the. . .other confederates did shortlye after the marriage. . .Combyne and Con-
Rafe Savidge
federate themselves to & with the said Willm Rowley (*blank*)
Aron Holland Thomas ffuller clerk
decker ^ and Richard Hodskyns and to and with diuers other
persons to your. . .Attorney as yet vnknowne, whose names he
prayeth may be inserted into this Informacion when they shalbe
discovered, which persons as well knowen as unknowne being
Combyned & Confederated to and with. . .Tobyas Audley and
the. . .other Confederats the said Rowley, dickers, &. . .Hodskyns
did most vnlawfully & libellouslye to the great scandall & disgrace of. . .Anne Elsden make devise & contrive one scandalous
enterlude or play most tauntinglye nameing the same enterlude
or play Keepe the widdowe wakeinge thereby setting forth and
intymateing how long. . .Ann Elsden was kept wakeinge, and
the maner of. . .Anne Elsdens distemperature with wyne and
hott waters and the losse of her estate. . .to the great infamy &
scandall of. . .Anne Elsden.

It is evident from this that, whether or no Audley and his
crew were the instigators, a play and ballad were the outcome of the marriage, and that this play was called *Keep the
Widow Waking*. There is, as a fact, no indication of their
complicity, which is alleged by the prosecution only in order
to involve Dekker and the other theatre people in a conspiracy, and so to bring them under the jurisdiction of the
Star Chamber. They are accused, in short, of a conspiracy
to libel Anne Elsdon. In the same way, Chapman, Woodford and Peers had been accused of conspiring to thwart
the ends of justice, when they were only turning a reasonably
honest penny by means of the topical drama, in *The Old
Joiner of Aldgate*.

It is clear from the three different handwritings of the original Bill and the interlined names, as also from the third recital of the names of the persons concerned, to which there are no additions, that Rowley, Dekker and 'Hodskyns' were the authors first cited, that Rafe Savage was added at one stage, and Aaron Holland and Thomas Fuller at another, in an uncertain order of priority, as further information became available for the prosecution. Of these persons, Hodgkins may for the moment be neglected, as it will appear that he was the author of the ballad and does not seem to have had any hand in the play. We are left then with Rowley and Dekker as its principal authors.

The final recital, at the end of the Bill, of the defendants who are to be summoned to answer to the charges, after naming some of Audley's group, runs as follows:

...Robte Taylor Edmond Ward ∧ ffrancis Hollyday (Will: Carpen) [Rowley] (Ellis Worth) deckers Richard Hodskines....[1]

(above line: Aaron Holland Thomas ffuller cler)
(above line: ter   Wm Rowley Raphe Savidge)

I judge that the names of Holland and Fuller were interlined by the clerk who drew up the Bill, that Carpenter and Worth were next inserted by a second clerk in the blank spaces left for Christian names before *Rowley* and *deckers*, and that a third hand deleted *Rowley* and interlined *Wm Rowley* and *Raphe Savidge* in this order of events. The same hands, for the most part, interlined the same names in each case in the Bill, and the order is probably the same. Thus it seems that the information supplied by Garfield originally contained the names of Audley's crew, the names of the two principal dramatists, whose Christian names were unknown to him, and the name of the writer of the ballad.

To these were added the names of Aaron Holland and

---

[1] Round brackets indicate original blank spaces, filled in here in a different hand; square brackets indicate deletion. There was not room for the whole of *Carpenter*, and *ter* was interlined.

Thomas Fuller. Holland is well known to us through various accounts of cases in the Court of Requests given by Greenstreet, Fleay and Wallace, and I have found a later record of a case in the Court of Chancery in 1623/4 which concludes the story of his relations with the Red Bull, and recapitulates the incidents of his long struggle with Thomas Woodford, which he finally won. I can add, from various other records, that he was a Berkshire man, born in 1556, who became an innkeeper in London, and lived successively in Grays Inn Lane, in the Savoy, and in St James, Clerkenwell, between 1589 and 1624. It is clear that in his later years he became a man of substance, though in 1589 he was rated for subsidy at £3 and paid 5s. Holland owned the lease of the messuage known as the Red Bull, and built a theatre on vacant land which formed part of it. He sold some shares of the profits soon after the theatre was built, but continued to be an important partner himself, and was therefore cited for complicity in the production of *Keep the Widow Waking*. In the Chancery suit, however, I find that Holland in his Answer declares that he had sold not only all his share in the profits, but also his lease, before 6 November 1623, the date of his Answer, though he reserved a small annuity to be derived from the theatre during his life. I have not been able to find out in what capacity Fuller was involved. He was an Essex man, of Stebbing, as appears from his wife's deposition, and his wife testifies that he went with her to carry Cartmell's proposal for a compromise to Garfield, though Garfield himself says that a certain Mary Paine was the messenger, and came soon after the marriage. The Fullers went about Bartholomew-tide, i.e. about 24 August, according to Mrs Fuller. Probably there were two embassies. The names of Carpenter and Worth were next inserted by a second clerk. Ellis Worth is a well-known actor, and gave evidence before the Court. William Carpenter is also known from other sources as an actor, but is not referred to again in this case. It is evident that these two were selected to answer for the company that acted the play at the Red Bull, as stated in the Bill,

which...libellous and scandalous enterlude & play...being thus contriued & made...Audley...did to scandalize & disgrace... Anne Elsden & make her ridiculous to the world, cause & procure the...play or enterlude to be seuerall tymes acted & played at the playhouse called the Bull at Clarkenwell in the Countye of Middlesex by the players there....

Finally the name of Rafe Savage is added. Dekker informs the Court in his Deposition that Savage gave instructions to the dramatist for the writing of the play, and nothing is said about his status. There are, however, inferences to be drawn from the records of Henslowe's dealings, and those of Wood-ford with Chapman in the Star Chamber suit dealt with earlier in this book. It is further known that one Thomas Savage had dealings in the shares of the Globe theatre in 1599.[1] In this case it seems reasonable to assume that Rafe Savage was cited as the successor of Aaron Holland and the purchaser of his property in the Red Bull, when Holland's disposal of his interests became known to the prosecution. This Rafe Savage may well have been the son of Thomas Savage, and inherited from him associations with theatrical property. It is regrettable that no question was put concerning payment for the play. The reply might have enlightened us upon Rafe Savage. One may take it for granted that he paid for it.

The net of the prosecution was evidently thrown widely to bring before the Court persons interested in the production of the play in all conceivable functions. It is evident from the Interrogatories that even attendance as a spectator was looked upon as evidence of complicity.

Of the persons cited Answers are entered and Depositions made by Worth, Holland, and Dekker only of the stage people. It is reasonable to suppose that Rowley was not examined because he had died before the case had proceeded

[1] E. K. Chambers, *Elizabethan Stage*, II. 417.

beyond the pleadings. In the Bill of Information, dated 26 November 1624, he is cited to appear as a defendant, but the words 'now dead' have been interlined in another hand after his name. There is no answer by Rowley, though Answers were sworn to by Worth on 31 January 1624/5, by Dekker on 3 February, and by Holland on 5 February. In Dekker's Deposition the following occurs—'John Webster [deceased] Willm Rowly John fford and this defendant', the word 'deceased' having been deleted. I have little doubt that the clerk, having correctly removed the word as referring to Webster, omitted to reinsert it in its proper place after 'Rowly', and that we may therefore date Rowley's death before Dekker's examination on 24 March 1625/6. Finally, in the Parish Registers of St James, Clerkenwell, the burial of 'William Rowley housekeeper' is recorded under date 11 February 1625/6, and we may reasonably accept this entry as referring to the actor-dramatist and fixing the date of his death.[1] Rowley may not have been called upon to enter an answer, but if he did so it would probably, after his death, be removed from the file of documents.

The aspect of the events which formed the staple of the play is defined by the title *Keep the Widow Waking*, and is illustrated in the concluding passage of the indictment quoted on pp. 97–8 above. The play made mirth of the protracted revels of Anne Elsdon with Audley and his companions, of his marriage to her, and of his seizure of her estate. The way in which the plot was worked out becomes clear from the ballad, which fortunately is quoted in full in the Bill, where

---

[1] *Harl. Soc. Publ.* vol. IV. It is known that Dekker's burial is recorded there also, on 25 August 1632. I am tempted to suggest that another of the four men engaged on this play for the Red Bull is referred to in a further entry, which records the burial of John Webster on 3 March 1637/8. The well-known reference in Heywood's *Hierarchie of the Angels* (1635 'Fletcher and Webster...neither was but Jacke') is not conclusive to the contrary. Fletcher had died in 1625, and this alone would determine the tense of the verb, unless Heywood were prepared to write 'Fletcher and Webster...neither was nor is respectively but Jacke'!

it is, of course, not arranged in lines, as in the following transcript, but is run on.

keeping the widow wakeing
or

lett him that is poore and to wealth would aspire
gett some old rich widdowe and grow wealthye by her,
to the tune of the blazing torch,

Yow yong men whoe would marrye well,
but are through want restrain'd,
Come list to that which I shall tell,
of one who wealth obtayn'd,
by wedding of a widow rich
all poore yong girles forsakeing,
he got this prize his hap was such,
to keepe the widow wakeing.

This widowe as I sayd before,
in treasure much abounded,
of gold & siluer she had store,
which many suitors wounded,
More then the darts of *Venus* boy,
yet she them all forsakeing,
kept it for him who had this toy,
to keepe the widdow wakeing.

The suitors were in nomber three,
that to this widowe went,
And each one stroue who should be he,
could give her best content,
One was a broker by his trade,
and liu'ed by Pawnes takeing,
He had noe lucke though he assayed,
to keepe the widow wakeing.

The second was a Horse Courser,
whose stocke lay all in Iadges,[1]
he thought to match him selfe with her,
thus wealth his mynd perswades,

[1] *sic=Jades.*

The third would wyn with sweete words,
he practiz't Comfit makeing,
But all his wit noe tricke affords
to keepe the widowe wakeing,

Although he profered loue to her,
t'was gold he most affected,
for wealth will withered age prefere,
when youth that is poore reiected.
yet while they to effect this match,
refused noe paines takeing,
another quicklye did dispatch
to keepe the widow wakeing,

ffor while those three and many more,
long tyme had wooed by guifts,
A young man that was verie poore,
and liued by spend thrifts,
which to his house resorted still,
Tobacco daylye taking,
He first of all devised this shifte,
to keepe the widow wakeing,

This yong man who thus liued by fume,
when he heard all this doeing,
A gallant state he did assume
And to her wen[1] a wooing.
Thought he if I can gett this prise,
t'will suerly be my making
Then he this Crochet did devise,
to keep the widow wakeing,

But better is two heads then one,
bout such a weightye matter,
Therefore he would not goe alone,
but ere that he came at her,
He wiselye tooke with him along,
lest he should faile through speakeing,
A Lawyer with a nimble tongue,
who kept the widow wakeing.

[1] *sic = went.*

Thus like a Gallant in array,
with his fine smooth tongu'd tutor,
He to the widow went that day,
and kindly did salute her,
Into a Taverne he her got,
where with much merry makeing.
In litle tyme they fayled not,
to keepe the widdow wakeing.

The second parte of which libellous Ballett, followeth in
these words.

Nowe they that rightlye would conceiue,
the meaning of this phrase,
Marke what ensues, & then perceiue,
The sequell all bewrayes,
The widow being plyed with wyne,
vntill her braynes were akeing,
she married was in such a vaine,
t'was hard to keepe her wakeing.

This yong man wiselye did invent,
before he went about her,
to frustrate each impediment,
might make him goe without her,
A priest he had provided there
who got her in that takeing,
That shee agreed they married were,
for which they kept her wakeing,

ffor hauing as is said before
transformed himselfe soe strange,
He like a Gentleman did rore,
I n'ere saw such a Change,
He that before to light the smoke,
with Coales for fire was rakeing.
Had now got on a Veluet Cloake,
to keepe the widdow wakeing.

There he decla'rd what land he had,
both arrable & meadow,
which did reioyce & make full glad,
the hart of this old widdowe,

To thinke that such a braue yong man,
should keepe her hart from akeing,
Her head was light, her tongue still ran,
whoe keeps the widow wakeing.

The yong man did noe tyme delay,
but quicklye did dispatch,
The priest some certaine words did say,
and soe made vpp the match,
Thus in foure howers the youth was sped,
in such a mood her takeing,
They wo'od, were married went to bed
to keepe the widow wakeing,

The other Suitors hearing all,
How they were thus defeated,
Their furye was I thinke not small,
to see them selues thus Cheated,
Yet could they not tell who to blame,
but her for them off shakeing,
They lost their time another came,
and kept the widow wakeing.

The new wife comeinge to her selfe,
did finde she was deceaued,
And that he tooke her more for pelfe,
then loue she well perceaued.
O prethee peace (quoth he) good wife)[1]
twas but a small mistakeing.
Ile be a comfort all thy life
a nights to keepe the wakeing.

Thus sometimes that haps in an houre,
that comes not in seauen yeare,
Therefore lett yong men that are poore,
come take example here,
And you whoe faine would heare the full
discourse of this match makeing,
The play will teach you at the Bull,
to keepe the widdow wakeing.

[1] *sic.*

This ballad, written after the play, purports to relate its plot, and instructs its hearers or readers that the story is to be had more in detail at the Bull. And there is no good reason for refusing its evidence, even though it be an advertisement.

It is abundantly evident, from the ballad, from the title of the play, and from Garfield's accusations, that the story of the marriage was treated in a facetious manner, with satirically frank insistence upon an old widow's appreciation of the attentions of a young husband and upon her convivial tendencies. The persons of the drama presumably included the three unsuccessful suitors, the broker, the horse-courser, and the comfit-maker, as well as Toby Audley, who is easily recognizable as a tobacco-seller. The Lawyer is probably Edmond Ward, who described himself to the Middlesex Justices as 'of the Inner Temple', though he is not to be found in its records. The priest is obviously Nicholas Cartmell. It was a strange fate indeed that brought the old Vicar of a charming and remote country village upon the boards of the Red Bull in the roaring streets of Clerkenwell. Circumstance and accident combined in the bizarre logic of this translation.

Nicholas Cartmell was born in 1546, entered Trinity College, Cambridge as a sizar in 1566, but took no degree, was ordained deacon in 1567 and priest in 1568, became Rector of Coton in 1571 and Vicar of Guilsborough in 1587, and held both cures until his death. He was thrice married, had a number of children, married four daughters well, set his Parish Registers in order, rebuilt his church in 1618, and in general seems to have been of an active and busy disposition. He had one son, also Nicholas, who became Vicar of Daventry in 1623 at the age of thirty-four, and in the year of his father's troubles. Garfield, confusing the father and the son, mentions Daventry as Cartmell's cure.

Cartmell, unfortunately, borrowed money from his son-in-law Hugh Bletsoe, his daughter Sara and his grandson Thomas, in 1611 and again in 1616, and got out of his depth. The end of it was a couple of Chancery suits in which he sought escape from his debts and which brought him up to London in 1622, in desperate straits for money in his old age, and an easy prey to evil influences. He was then seventy-six years of age, and perhaps more to be pitied than to be blamed. I suspect that he borrowed money for the repair of his church, and so was brought to play this lamentable part in our story. In the end he returned to Guilsborough, made his will on 3 January 1626, leaving an estate worth about £250, and was buried there six days later.

Garfield does not appear in the ballad as the widow's son-in-law, nor does her daughter appear. The ballad confines itself to the widow and her suitors. It is evident that the dramatic effect would be vastly improved if the wooing were carried on in despite of interested relatives and were accompanied by their chorus of dismay. But the play had to be limited by the exigencies of its double plot, and it may be that this theme was lightly handled. Or Garfield might possibly have been merged into one of the suitors, and thus his anger at the marriage might have been readily fitted into the comic plot. It may well be imagined that an actor could make up to resemble him closely enough to add zest to the impersonation. And it could then be argued in defence of the play that it was not a libel upon Garfield, the circumstances not corresponding. But it could only be with real regret that Dekker and the actors would resort to this device and deviate from the superior comedy of real life. We may be reasonably certain, at any rate, that both Garfield and Cartmell, as well as the other principal persons, appeared on the stage in shapes recognizable to the initiated, that is, to all Clerkenwell at least.

We may assume that the play concludes with the success of the plot, the widow making the best of a bad bargain, as many a deceived bride or bridegroom has to do in Elizabethan plays. The moral appears to be that poor young men should try to follow in Audley's cozening footsteps. The widow deserved what she got for her unseemly conduct and

for marrying a young man. Such marriages were frequent
enough to be a sore point with the youth of London, and
the popular drama often deals faithfully with them. There is
no attempt here, it will be observed, to disguise the fact that
this marriage was in some measure fraudulent. But Audley
was undoubtedly the hero of the plot, a young apprentice-
gallant who scored off the Philistines.

Further information about the action of the play is available in the Interrogatories and in the evidence given. It is
clear that it showed Audley and Hide discussing the procuring
of the licence of marriage. Audley in a vein of mirth narrates
how he told the officials 'that it was for an old bedd ridden
woman and a young fellow together'. There is, again, a
tavern scene. Here the widow is drinking with her suitor
and his friends, when a drawer enters, dressed as a girl, with
an empty basket, pretending to bring in a basket of apricots
from one of the widow's tenants as a present for her. Thereupon some one calls for wine, knocking on the table with a
pot. The drawer forgets his role and answers 'Anon, anon,
Sir'. This joke at Anne's expense is, of course, planned by
Audley and his friends, probably after the marriage, when
they are elated with their success and somewhat less defer-
ential to the trapped widow.

In both instances these scenes repeated on the stage actual
incidents that had taken place, and both must have been
unpleasant for Anne or her family to hear about. Nor would
they appreciate Audley coming upon the stage with an armful
of 'wrightings' or deeds, conveyed from Anne's house and
shown in triumph to the rest of the crew. I gather that
Garfield did not actually see the play, but Snowe did, and
relates what he saw. Most of the defendants either denied
having seen it, or fought shy of remembering it. Dekker
testified that he 'did often see the...play or parte thereof
acted but how often he cannot depose'. He describes the
Apricot Episode, and admits vaguely 'some passage acted
in the...play about the getting of a license for the mariage

of the widow there personated'. He is the only person who admits that he commended the play, though not excessively. But then he was one of the authors.

§ v. DRAMATISTS AND ACTORS AT WORK

'Writing some parte of the...play himself (he) dyd perchance let fall some words thereabouts', Dekker told the Court. In his Answer he had defined his share in the play. It consisted of 'two sheetes of paper conteyning the first Act' of the play 'and a speech in the last Scene of the last Act of the Boy who had killed his mother'. This speech would surely be the dying oration of Nathaniel Tindall at the time of his execution, of which doubtless something remains in the extant Ballad of Tindall's repentance. The illustrations of this broadside are our only other possible source of information concerning this part of the play, except for the records of the Old Bailey. Dekker had also given the full title of the play as *The late Murder in White Chappell*, or *Keepe the Widow waking*. In his Deposition he informed the Court that he, together with John Webster, William Rowley and John Ford made and contrived the play 'vppon the instructions giuen them by one Raph Savage'. This evidence is confirmed by Ellis Worth's Deposition, of which the following is a transcript in part:

17....hee did not, nor knoweth that anie other did, in derision of...Anne Ellesden, in the Taverne...putt a boy into Wenches apparrell, and cause him with an emptie baskett to tell...Anne that hee had brought a baskett of apricocks from one of her Tenants neither did hee...neither doth hee know that anie other did...knocke with a pott, and vpon the same knocking a boy of the...howse answere anon anon Sir neither doth hee...know whether such manner of knocking with a pott, and answering anon anon Sir hath bin since acted vpon the Stage at the Redd Bull, when the play called *Keepe the widow waking* hath bin acted, or played, ffor that hee...neuer played in the same play, nor sawe the same.

18. ...hee was not privie to, or present at the sueing out of the license for the marrieing of...Tobias Awdley and...Anne Ellesden, nor doth know that any one which procured the said license did say, that it was for the marrieing of an old bedd ridden woman and a young fellow together. neither doth hee...know whether anie such thing hath bin acted in the...play at the Redd Bull or not, for that hee...never sawe the same play.

27. ...hee was not acquainted with, nor had anie hand in the contriving acting or playing of the foresaied play *called:* called (keepe the widow waking) nor can of his *the murder of* owne knowledge say [by whom by name the *the woman in* saied play was contrived nor] who gave in-*white Chappell* struccons for the contriving thereof But he be-*by her sonne or* leiveth [it was contrived and writ] that the play *Keepe the* [intended by the Int] was contrived and written *widow waking* by Wm Rowley, Jon ffoord, John Webster, and +Tho: +[neither] doth not [hee this Defendant] know Decker+and how often the same play hath been acted or this def played at the Redd Bull in Saint Johns Street, further saieth neither did hee this defendant ever see the same that hee play acted or played, nor did drawe anie other so to doe, nor hath much comended of the saied play.[1]

One cannot be certain of the precise significance of Dekker's 'two sheets of paper' containing a whole act, and a speech of another act. Two sheets means four leaves or eight pages, as for example in the sheets numbered by the author in Massinger's MS. play *Believe as you List* (1631). Eight pages are by no means necessarily inadequate for a complete Act of a play. It is true that the average length of an act in the fourteen full-length plays in MS. Egerton 1994 is 9·1 pages. But of these plays nine have one or more acts

[1] I have given this extraordinary reply as it stands. It suggests hesitation on Worth's part, and pressing by prosecuting counsel. Did Worth try to keep Dekker out of it? The order of the middle part is as follows: 'the play was contrived and written by Wm Rowley, Jon ffoord, John Webster, and Tho: Decker and this def further saieth that hee doth not know how often etc.' Square brackets mark deletions here, as elsewhere.

covering less than eight pages. Seventeen acts are written on less than eight pages, of which ten cover less than seven pages, and five less than six pages. The shortest of the plays, *Charlemagne*, averages 6·8 pages for all five acts.

Presumably Dekker meant two consecutive sheets on which he wrote the whole of his contribution. He would hardly have referred to his share in these words if he meant that he had written the first act, and had also written a page or two pages in continuation of another man's copy. It is most likely that he wrote the first act on the first six pages, and the separate speech on the last leaf which could be detached and inserted in its proper place, when the play was assembled.

This would seem to indicate that the play was jobbed out to the four authors in detached acts, with one important passage at least reserved for special treatment. The fact that four authors were engaged on the play strengthens this presumption. Doubtless the need for rapid production dictated this multiplicity of authorship, and precluded anything in the shape of close continuous collaboration between all four.[1] It is reasonable to assume then that Dekker and Rowley, the original defendants, worked out the plot together, then called Webster and Ford into consultation, and apportioned the acts. I imagine that a pretty complete scenario would be presented by Dekker and Rowley, with sufficient summaries of the action of each act for the needs of the various authors.[2] Dekker, I take it, had completed the first act, and so introduced the persons of the play and given them their characters. This would be read to the other three, who would thus be enabled to carry on separately with the help of their sum-

---

[1] The date of the licence of the finished play was probably between 3 September and 15 September 1624. The 'marriage' took place at the end of July. The authors had at the outside a month in which to write the play.

[2] There is an example of such a possible summary in the manuscript play *Bonduca*, where it is inserted by the scribe who copied it out in place of a missing scene (B.M. Add. MS. 36758).

maries. It is possible, indeed, that the scenario took the form
of a complete Plot or Platt, but such documents represent
a later stage in the production of a play, and the existing
examples do not contain the information necessary for the
writing of the play.

We have observed that Dekker himself wrote the first
act, and wrote one speech by Tindall in the fifth act. It
follows that Dekker contributed to both the tragic plot
and the comic, unless the first act dealt exclusively with the
murder plot, which is most unlikely, and is moreover in-
consistent with Dekker's appearance as a defendant and with
his evidence. This fact is significant, for it opposes the
common assumption that in collaboration the comic part was
assigned to one author and the tragic to another. A great deal
of guesswork has been based on this assumption, in proposed
allotments of parts of printed plays to their various collabor-
ating authors.

One cannot help wondering how far the authors were
bound by their 'instructions', which they received from
Savage. Considering who Savage probably was, and bearing
in mind the evidence of Worth and Dekker, it seems clear
that the instructions were of a general nature. It is explicitly
stated that the play was 'contrived and writ' (Worth) by
the four playwrights, that some one 'gave instructions for
the contriving thereof' (Worth). The distinction between
plotting and writing is here preserved, and both were the
business of the dramatists. Savage may, of course, have
supplied information about actual incidents, as well as the
general order to put the marriage and the murder into a play
for the Red Bull. But the question of the actors available
would probably have more effect in the working out of the
play than Savage's views, if he had any. And Dekker and
Rowley were probably well in touch with local gossip.
There is no indication that the business men who invested
in theatre property had necessarily any interest in the
dramatic or literary aspect of their concerns. Henslowe is

not the only example. Woodford, who paid Chapman for his play for the Children of Paul's, was a busy merchant who even went overseas and left his interests in charge of a substitute. Holland was almost illiterate, as appears from his own statement in the Chancery suit mentioned above, and from his scrawled signature in initials only.

Finally, it seems probable that Dekker, who wrote the first act and so introduced the stories and the characters, who reserved for himself the outstanding opportunity offered by the murder plot, and who alone appeared before the Court, was the principal agent in the making of the play and was entrusted with its execution. Rowley, as we shall see, was at this time a member of the company of Prince Charles, and Dekker was a free lance.

Thus the play was written. It was then taken to the Master of the Revels to be licensed. Sir Henry Herbert succeeded Sir John Astley in the Mastership on 20 July 1623, farming the office from him for £150 a year. The entry in his office book relating to this play is thus recorded in Chalmers's *Supplemental Apology*.

1624 September 'A New Tragedy, called, A Late Murther of the Sonn upon the Mother: Written by Forde, and Webster'.

The preceding entry is dated 3 September and the succeeding entry 15 September, so that we may presume the licence to have been given between these two dates.

It is obvious that this licence arouses questions. Why is there no mention of the alternative title *Keep the Widow Waking*, and no mention of Dekker and Rowley? It might be argued that only the murder part of the play was submitted, and that Ford and Webster were the authors of this part and Rowley and Dekker of the comic part. Yet we know that Dekker, as a fact, wrote part of the murder plot. The title, again, as given by Herbert, does not tally with that given by either Worth or Dekker, but is closely similar to that of the ballad. It is common enough for Herbert's record to omit the second or alternative title of a play, and it is reasonable to suggest that he did not enter the names of all the authors, if indeed they were all mentioned on the copy. Worth's enumeration of the authors puts Dekker's name last, and possibly the order of names that reached Herbert had Ford and Webster first. Possibly even he knew their names better, as being writers for the King's Company with its great prestige. Certainly, to take the licence at its face value involves impossibilities. The murder story could not have been sent up separately for licence under the names of Ford and Webster only, and at least half of the play acted without licence. Dekker, in his defence, definitely claims that the whole play was licensed by Herbert. No conclusion can reasonably be drawn from the wording of the licence, especially in view of what happened subsequently.

When the play was first acted at the Red Bull, Garfield was charged by Anne Elsdon to go to the Deputy Master of the Revels with a petition to him to prohibit the performance of the play of which rumours were abroad. He accordingly went to William Blagrave, and paid him twenty shillings, 'the vsuall ffee for allowing of a play as (Garfield) was informed'. Garfield's idea was evidently that he was more likely to get justice if the official concerned were assured against losing by his sense of justice. The Deputy, in fact, promised to forbid the play. Nevertheless Herbert allowed it, and it was acted. Thus the net result of the petition was to double the fees of the Office of the Revels, and the conclusion was satisfactory to all but Garfield and Anne Elsdon. Garfield subsequently appealed to Worth and the other Red Bull players 'to forbeare to act the...play which notwithstandinge was often acted afterwards'. They knew that they had nothing to fear from the Master of the Revels or the Lord Chamberlain. The Master was, by force of circumstances, the natural ally of the players, for their interests coincided. The theatres were the main source of the considerable income that Herbert derived from his office, and he was not the man to allow the prosperity of the theatre, and consequently his own prosperity, to be interfered with, except when higher authority might be involved. As for Blagrave's acceptance of the twenty shillings and his promise to forbid the play, we may perhaps find a parallel in Mr Spenlow. 'I will not say what consideration I might give to the point myself, Mr Copperfield, if I were unfettered. Mr Jorkins is immovable.' Garfield at any rate gave him up, and went on an equally hopeless quest to the players.

One is moved to suspicion also concerning the ballad. It is clearly an advertisement of the play, arousing curiosity about its contents and explicitly inciting the reader or hearer to visit the Red Bull to see the play. John Griffin heard the ballad sung in the streets. Garfield testifies that it was

repeated and sung by a ballad monger vnder the windowe of... Anne Ellesden which balladmonger was brought before Geo: Longe Esq one of the Justices of the Peace for the County of Middlesex who Comitted him to prison for that yt appeared vppon his examinacion he was purposely sent thither to singe the said ballad by one Holland.

Holland was duly interrogated on this point, and his reply must have enlivened an already lively case. He enters a complete denial of all complicity in the matter, and even all knowledge of the matter. He certainly did not

cause or procure the first or second parte of the...ballett to bee sung or read vnder or neere the Chamber window of...Anne Ellesden only this defendant saieth, that hee...coming one day out of one Dugdale's[1] howse a Chandler in Clerkenwell Close, there was a fellow that had bin singing of balletts thereabouts (as it seemed) and carried balletts about him which spake vnto him ...and asked him, if hee would buy the ballett of *Keepe the widow waking*, and this defendant seeing him to be a lustie fellow, and

---

[1] Probably the William Dugdale who was a witness to Garfield's will in 1630. John Davis, a dyer and therefore a fellow-craftsman in Garfield's former trade, who gave evidence here for the prosecution, was another witness to the will. Dugdale also was one of Audley's prosecutors before the Middlesex Sessions.

fitt for labour, grew angrie with him, and much blamed and reprehended him, that being so strong and able a person, hee followed so idle a course of life as selling & singing of balletts vpp and downe the streets and tould him if hee were well seru'd hee should bee punish'd & sett to worke and the saied fellow making answer that hee would sell & sing balletts, notwithstanding what hee this defendant saied to the contrarie, or words to that effect, hee this defendant replied, in theis or like words, well, sing on, thou mayest happen to be well paied for thy paines. this defendant meaning thereby, that because it was neere the howse of Correccion, some Constable or other officer would take notice of him as an idle person, and have him to the howse of Correccion.

With these disconcertingly righteous words the old gentleman concluded his evidence, and held on indignantly back to the other shy traffickers.

John Griffin was more helpful, for he

did heare a ballad sang in the streetes called keepe the widow waking and...did heare a stranger whose name was Richard but what more he knoweth not say that he made the...ballad being at a play and did after he had seene the...play make the ballad before he slept and this defendant saith the said person did dwell neer Ste Pulichers church and was a booke seller.[1]

With Griffin's evidence, and with our knowledge that Richard Hodgkins was concerned with John Trundle in the Murder Ballads, we need not question Hodgkins's authorship of this ballad, of which he is accused in the Bill. And it is not unreasonable to believe that those who drew dividends from the Red Bull might well evince their gratitude for a good advertisement. It is also reasonable to conceive that in any case the best place for singing or selling the ballad was near Anne Elsdon's house, where there would be for some time a concourse of the curious, and where the ballad would make its strongest appeal to malicious tattlers. Garfield complained 'that 2 play boyes of the...Red Bull passing

---

[1] *Deposition of John Griffin*, 'Tailor, of St. Buttolph near Aldersgate', aged thirty-two.

by this deponents house [one] pointinge therat to his fellowe saide there dwelte the widdowe waking'. The phrase must have had quite an intense local currency for a time, as a catchword of deplorable possibilities. It had long been in occasional proverbial use. And Dr G. B. Harrison[1] found an instance of its occurrence in remarkably similar circumstances, when a certain Mrs Mescall, a sexagenarian 'Tripe-wife' of means, went through experiences which offer a close parallel to those of Mrs Elsdon, some thirty years before, in 1595. The story is told in a pamphlet entitled *A quest of Enquirie*, reprinted by Grosart, and in two ballads, the first of which is reprinted in Professor Baskervill's *Elizabethan Jig*. This ballad reflects once more the close connection between the London stage and the current scandals of the day, and suggests the probability that the players will make a jig of the affair:

> The trimming of the Tripe wife:
> it makes me in a rage,
> And doubt least that the players
> will sing it on the stage.

The spread of the catchword used by the play for its title, and by Hodgkins as the refrain of his ballad, would be considerably favoured by its proverbial history and by memories of this scandal of the past.

Richard Hodgkins seems to have become free of the Company of Stationers on 4 April 1624, and to have registered his first publication on 2 July 1624.[2] The Murder Ballad that is extant is entered to Hodgkins but bears the imprint

---

[1] *The Library*, June 1930, pp. 97–101.

[2] Hodgkins eludes me, apart from this. There was a 'Richard Hodgkins a pore man', buried at St James, Clerkenwell, on 28 September 1630, and 'Elline, d. of Richard Hodgkyns', on 24 September 1630, during the plague of this year. There was a John Hodgkins concerned in the Marprelate printing in 1589. And one Richard Hotchekins was a beneficiary, along with William Seres, probably the Stationer, under the will of Edward Heminge, a connexion of John Day the printer, which was proved on 27 July 1604.

'Printed at London for John Trundle'.[1] The second was entered to both Trundle and Hodgkins, and was written by John Morgan. The Marriage Ballad is extant only in the Bill, where the imprint is not given, and it was not entered in the Register. It certainly was printed and offered for sale, however, as we have seen.

I can only touch here upon one of the questions that arise out of these facts. It is probable that the Master of the Revels connived at the printing of it. Add. MS. 19356 in the British Museum contains a document dated 25 July 1663, which argues that not only plays but ballads should come under the jurisdiction of the Master who should license ballads for printing as he licenses plays for acting. The author of this document, Edward Hayward, then Herbert's Deputy, made further Notes of Inquiries to be made of the Master, dated 27 July 1663, which are preserved in the same MS. In this document, he notes,

Md. old Mr Whitehead affirmes, that all Comedies, Tragedies, Poems, Ballads, half sides, drolleries, and all billes relating to Jokes belongs to the Reuells, & were soe accompted in the times of Queen Elizabeth and King James, and further sayes that to his knowledge Edward Walker formerly servant to Sir Henry tooke moneyes for concealing many of the particulars last mentioned.[2]

Certainly Herbert had, soon after he became Master, confirmed Buc's claim to license plays for printing, and had gone far to establish a new claim to license poetry for printing (as the Stationers' Registers bear witness), and to receive fees for so doing. Nor was poetry licensed by him always registered, as in the case of Cowley's first boyish efforts, in 1632.[3]

It is possible that Hodgkins foresaw a refusal of the

---

[1] No. 210 in the same collection of Ballads in the Library of the Society of Antiquaries has the imprint 'Printed at London for John Trundle, and are to be sold at his shop neere the Hospitall Gate 1624'.

[2] Fol. 78.

[3] J. Q. Adams, *Dramatic Records of Sir Henry Herbert*, p. 41.

Stationers' Company, and was prepared to allege the licence of the Lord Chamberlain through his representative the Master of the Revels, without entering the ballad in the Register. Possibly Walker, the Clerk to the Office of the Revels, took upon him the Royal authority for the nonce, and had his fee in respect of the ballad, as the Master and the Deputy had each had theirs in respect of the play. Clerks were important persons, in any case, and were worth mollifying. The Clerks in the Court of Chancery, for example, had regular fees, which I have seen entered in lawyers' notes of expenses of this period. Truly, Garfield had to contend with strong vested interests.

All manner of payments from the theatres to the Master of the Revels bound him to their service. Fees for the licensing of theatres, annual fees, benefit performances, and fees for licensing and 'reforming' plays, would all make an emissary from a theatre find open doors and a welcome, whereas Garfield's visit portended a diminution in the flow of receipts. What Jupiter but would frown upon one who would rob his altars! The long drawn-out Chancery suit of *Worth* v. *Baskerville*, in which in its final stages Herbert became arbitrator, suggests some abuse by him of his position in favour of the actors Worth and Blaney about a year later.

I will only add further concerning the ballad, that the account here given of the writing of it, and of its relation to the play, is of great interest. It is fair to assume that we see here the normal course of events when the notoriety of the subject was due mainly to its representation upon the stage. Thus in this instance the Murder Ballads preceded the play, and the Marriage Ballad was founded upon it and succeeded it. One need not, I think, hesitate to imagine that the writer of the ballad of *King Leir and his Three Daughters* had actually been present at the Globe before he wrote it, even if he did not necessarily eschew sleep until it was finished. Nor need we assume that the King's Players would scorn the valuable services of ballad writers and balladmongers who called attention to plays in course of production in their theatre. It would be the most effective form of advertisement then available.

It remains for me to attempt to answer a question that seems to have baffled Garfield, the question who acted the play. Of the actors mentioned in the case, the actor-dramatist William Rowley is known to have been a member of Prince Charles's Company without break from 1610 to 1625. William Carpenter was also of this company in 1625, and almost certainly in 1619, and probably throughout the period between these dates.[1] It is further known that this company, which had hitherto been at the Curtain, acted at the Red Bull on 19 August 1623, and apparently left the Curtain for good some time after 10 June 1623. They remained at the Red Bull until 1625, when some of the company, being Prince Charles's men, were naturally taken over into the new King's players, while the rest joined with others to form the new Red Bull Company.

Ellis Worth is known to have been a member of Queen Anne's Company from 1612, and of the same company, after the death of the Queen in 1619, under its new name the Children of the Revels or the Players of the Revels, in May 1623. It had occupied the Red Bull from the date of its opening, between 1604 and 1606, up to 1623. But now Worth had to seek new associates elsewhere. It is known that later in 1623 this old Red Bull Company had left the theatre and had broken up, as a result of the steady drain upon their profits resulting from the agreement made in 1616 to pay Mrs Baskerville 3s. 8d. a day. It seemed their only hope of evading this obligation.[2] In 1631 we find Worth an important member of the Palsgrave's Company, after it had been taken into the service of the infant Prince

---

[1] He was a member of the Lady Elizabeth's Company in 1611.
[2] I hope some day to give a full account of these happenings, based on new documents in the Record Office which supplement those printed in Fleay (*Stage*, pp. 270 ff.).

Charles (Charles II). From 1623 to 1632 this company occupied the Fortune. They eventually migrated to the Red Bull, and Worth with them, but not until 1635 probably. It is very likely that Worth joined them at the Fortune as soon as he could, but it is impossible to say how long before 1631 he was taken in. He certainly had to leave the Red Bull in 1623, in order to strengthen his defence against Mrs Baskerville's claims.

It would appear probable enough, therefore, that Worth was speaking the truth when he deposed that he had had nothing to do with the play, and had not even seen it acted. It would also appear probable that the other guess of the prosecution was nearer the truth. If Carpenter himself did not actually take a part in the play, it was probably Prince Charles's Company, of which he was a member, that produced it. The suggestion is strengthened by the fact that Rowley, another member of this company, was part author. His intimate knowledge of the company would help greatly in the writing of the play, in fitting the characters to the actors available and their special gifts.

There are, however, other possibilities. Herbert's record of the licence of the play comes immediately after the licence of *The Captive*, by Heywood, to the Cockpit Company, the Lady Elizabeth's men. It is not stated for which company it was licensed, and Adams therefore suggests that it was licensed to the Cockpit Company[1] (among whom, by the way, were Christopher Beeston and Heywood, former Red Bull men). But there is no reason for accepting this as in any way probable.

We must take into account again the fact that plays were acted at the Red Bull by unknown companies. For example, on 18 September 1623 a play by Day was licensed by Herbert as 'For a Company of Strangers', at the Red Bull. It seems clear that this play was in fact by Day and Dekker, so that we have Dekker writing for an outside company for

[1] J. Q. Adams, *Dramatic Records of Sir Henry Herbert*, p. 29, n. 4.

this theatre a year before. A similar entry for 28 November 1623 licenses *The Faiyre fowle one*, by (William?) Smith, 'for a Strange Company at the Red Bull'. A play of popular sort, Wentworth Smith's *The Hector of Germany*, had been acted in 1613 'at the Red Bull, and at the Curtaine, by a Companie of Young Men of this Citie', as the title-page of the printed play informs us. It would be delightful to imagine that *Keep the Widow Waking* was produced by an amateur dramatic society of young Clerkenwell heroes, but the evidence is against such a supposition. Herbert seems to make a point of mentioning such exceptions to the general rule, and to have refused to put his hand to the licence in such a case.

It is true that Carpenter seems to have dropped out of the prosecution after its initial stage, but possibly it was judged that it would be wiser not to attack an actor under the powerful protection of Prince Charles, which Rowley also enjoyed. Worth and Dekker were brought into Court. But Dekker was a free lance, and Worth was possibly still unattached.

So we are left to meditate upon the spectacle of an immense complicity of the owners of a great popular London theatre, of four of the most distinguished living dramatists, of an excellent company of actors, of high officials of the Crown, and of the people of Clerkenwell, in the production of a play which must have grievously hurt the feelings of some respectable citizens of London who had already suffered in mind, body, and estate from the events reflected in the play, and who sought redress on the whole in vain. Such things doubtless added one more count in the persistent and acrimonious charges levelled at the stage by the City, of which Garfield was no unworthy representative. He had made a fortune in his trade, and died a wealthy man, owning lands in London and in Leicestershire, and provided well for the three surviving grandchildren of Mrs Elsdon.[1]

It was a strange freak of fate that his eldest son, Benjamin

[1] His will (*Scroope* 97) is dated 3 November 1630.

Garfield the younger, should have meddled with the for-
bidden thing, and turned playwright, however literary his
intent. In 1650 a poem was addressed by one Robert Baron,
in a volume of verse entitled *Pocula Castalia*,

To my Honour'd Friend Benjamin Garfield Esq; Vpon his
excellent Tragi-Comedy Entitled The Vnfortunate Fortunate,

in which Baron asserts concerning plays

> They're sermons in disguise, a good Play is
> A lecture of humanity. So is this...
> Go forth, and live, great Master of thy Pen,
> And share the Lawrell with thy namesake Ben.

It was perhaps well that his other namesake Ben, his much
abused father, had long since settled firmly in his grave.

Chapter III

THE JIG

(i) *The Jig*

The public stage in London, with its professional companies of actors, does not exhaust the possibilities of dramatic material for suits for libel in the Court of Star Chamber during Shakespeare's lifetime. There are two further types of dramatic literature, which are hardly mentioned in histories of what might be called official literature, but which were widely practised, both in the provinces and in London, and from time to time emerged from their obscurity to exercise the minds of the Judges in that Court, and so to come upon record. The Jig and the May Game, indeed, in one way or another, were evidently a source of continual trouble to the officers of government and of justice throughout the Tudor period.

The Jig was a kind of entertainment whose history is at least as obscure as that of the May Game, but which is better known in a general way because of its close relation to the Elizabethan stage in London and to the literary drama. All readers of Shakespeare know, for example, how the play of *Twelfth Night* ends with a song sung by the Clown or jester, Feste, and how this song, probably accompanied by a dance, is taken as an example of the Jig which frequently followed a play as an after-piece on the public stage, just as in later centuries a pantomime came after the serious play to conclude the evening's entertainment. So again Shakespeare's *Henry the Fourth* ends with a humorous prose speech spoken by a dancer who appends a dance to his speech before kneeling down to pray for the Queen.

But it is clear that if this were the sum of our knowledge we should be at a loss to understand why the Middlesex Justices, on 1 October 1612, made an Order for Suppressing Jigs at the end of Plays. The Justices at their General Sessions noted complaints arising out of

certayne lewde Jigges songes and daunces vsed and accustomed at the play-house called the Fortune in Gouldinglane,

accompanied apparently by troubles caused by such entertainments, for

divers cutt-purses and other lewde and ill-disposed persons in greate multitudes doe resorte thither at th'end of euerye playe, many tymes causinge tumultes and outrages wherebye His Majesties peace is often broke and much mischiefe like to ensue thereby.

Why should disreputable people throng to a theatre, after the main play, to hear and see a concluding song and dance? Why should such shows cause tumults? And why should it be a question for such serious consideration by the governors of the City? This is the problem of which no solution has yet been demonstrated.

One of the difficulties is, of course, that no authentic example of the stage-Jig has survived in English other than such elementary songs and dances as we find at the end of *Twelfth Night*, in ballad form, or in simple dialogue form. Such things clearly are inoffensive. And the paucity of material is well exemplified by the forgery of a Jig by the indefatigable Collier. Nor can even Professor Baskervill, in his exhaustive work upon *The Elizabethan Jig*, exhibit a single Elizabethan or Jacobean Jig of a more elaborate kind which can be proved to have been a stage-Jig. Yet I am clear that several of those quoted were in fact of such a nature, especially what is known as *Attowell's Jig*,[1] which as printed bears the signature of George Attowell. For Attowell was a player in Lord Strange's company. This Jig has

[1] Another example is that printed in Clarke's *Shirburn Ballads* (pp. 354–60) under the title of *A proper new ballett, intituled Rowland's god-sonne*.

stage-directions of a simple sort, moreover, and it is in general a close parallel to a couple of Jigs which I have come across in libel suits, and which are certainly examples of stage-Jigs in the provinces.

The Jig in its origins was evidently a dance of a certain type, such as would come from popular use into the hands, and feet, of a professional entertainer, and so naturally come to be combined with a song or ballad as part of his show, accompanied by pipe and tabor. The ballad part of the entertainment developed into dialogue, one of the favourite themes of balladry being love and courting, with an elementary story or plot, with two singers and dancers in a duet. Given a small company of actors, all trained singers and dancers, the thing was bound to grow in their hands into a more complex form, and to develop into something of a short operetta. The analogy of the ordinary stage-play would hasten the process, when once the Jig had taken its place as an appendix to the play proper.

What then was the real trouble with the Jig? Why does Hamlet show such unmeasured contempt for a 'jig-maker'? After all, Shakespeare's own contemporary in the company, its comic star, William Kempe, was a jig-maker and a jig-dancer. And Kempe's great predecessor, Richard Tarlton, had been proverbially famous in the same quality. Certainly the Middlesex Justices speak of 'lewde jigs'. And the dramatist Dekker puts it more strongly, writing of 'a nasty bawdy jigge'. But indecency in itself was not a matter in Elizabethan days, unless it were outrageous, for administrative action. There are hints, however, of the true explanation. Cotgrave defines a farce as in one sense, 'the Jyg at the end of an Enterlude, wherein some pretie knauery is acted'. The printer, John Budge, who refused to print the Wells May Game rhyme, refused because he suspected some 'knavery' in it.[1] Henry Chettle, in *Kindheart's Dream*, defending the stage, and at-

---

[1] See below, p. 176.

tacking rival vices, represents London sharks complaining
of plays:

no sooner haue we a tricke of deceipt, but they (plays) make it
common, singing Iigs, and making jeasts of vs, that euerie boy
can point out our houses as they passe by.

It would seem that the stage-Jig took upon itself to introduce
into its songs criticisms of contemporary and topical matters
of a scandalous interest, and we may well begin to understand the attitude of Clerkenwell cut-throats, sharpers and
bullies, and the possibility of free fighting after or during
such a Jig on the Fortune stage. We need not be surprised,
moreover, to find the satirist Wither writing of

a Rime,
A Curtain Jigge, a Libell, or a Ballet

as products of the same type and spirit.

The fact is, surely, that the stage-Jig, in its full development, was one more form of libel or defamation, turning
to dramatic purpose such topical scandals as afforded material
for an evening's mirth and were likely to lead to breaches of
the peace by the persons offended and their sympathisers.
It is this, I think, that explains why the true home of this
kind of Jig, generally improper in its theme, was the theatres
of lower reputation, the Fortune, the Curtain, and the Red
Bull, and why we should beware of imagining that Shakespeare's company and the Globe or Blackfriars ever exhibited
the Jig in this form, at any rate. The dramatist and actor with
some pride in his art and his profession, who despised jig-
makers, surely shared the contempt of Marlowe, on literary
grounds also, for

jigging veins of rhyming mother-wits

who descended to this pandering to the lowest tastes of
London audiences.

The examples I shall cite have the great advantage that the
records of their origin furnish a full explanation and inter-

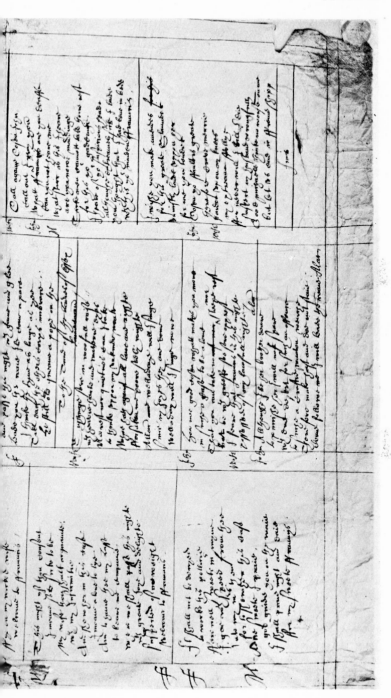

THE JIG OF *MICHAEL AND FRANCIS*

From *Star Chamber* 5, 30/16

pretation of the Jigs which came into writing and were presented on a stage, in one instance on a professional stage. From this we may with reasonable certainty conclude that some such facts of contemporary life underlie a London product like *Attowell's Jig*.

(ii) *Michael and Frances* in Yorkshire

§ i. A GOOD JEST

The short verse-play to which I have given the title of *Michael and Frances* has a special interest of its own. It is beyond all question a Jig, of the kind that was acted by stage-players as an after-piece, for it is acknowledged as a Jig in this sense by its victims and it was actually so performed. It is, therefore, of unique interest, for there is no other extant specimen of the kind with an equal claim to indisputable authority. Any definition of the Jig must take *Michael and Frances* into account. And we can well understand from reading it, and from considering its origin and its occasion, how its congeners on the London stage were likely to scandalize, or even to set by the ears, some of those who stayed, or trooped in after the play, to hear them.

The actors who are said to have adopted *Michael and Frances* for performance as an after-piece are those whose steps I have traced in Nidderdale and elsewhere, concerned in the acting of *St Christopher* and of certain plays of Shakespeare in 1609. Here we find the Simpsons' Company, a few years earlier, touring Yorkshire, and taking what opportunity was offered of profiting from local affairs in the exercise of their art.

The story of the events which gave birth to this Jig are not in themselves of any notable interest. It is an ordinary story of scandal arising possibly out of local animosities between two Yorkshiremen, Michael Steel of Skelton, between

Boroughbridge and Ripon, and Edward Meynell, the squire of Hawnby, in the wild country of the Cleveland Hills near Rievaulx, who held land also at Hilton and Normanby away in the North of the Riding. I do not know what line of dissension bridged the thirty-five miles between Skelton and Hawnby, far enough distant, one might have thought, for even two Yorkshiremen to have been able to live at peace in the same county. Whatever it was, Meynell thought fit to spread a slander concerning Steel and his maidservant Frances Thornton, raising a question whether she was in truth either a maid, or a servant in his house, and making no doubt of their illicit relations. The libel itself brings in John Thornton, a brother of Frances, who appears to be a cousin of Mrs Steel. But this does not help to explain any possible feud. Steel himself hints at earlier quarrels. Meynell and his associates put it all down to their appreciation of a good jest, which happened to be at the expense of Steel.

Steel at all events sought redress in the Council of the North, where he lodged his Bill on 18 June 1602, complaining of this attack upon his hitherto unblemished reputation. Meynell, together with his friend William Bowes of Ellerbeck and Francis Mitchell, Meynell's servant, were responsible for a libel which they had spread far and wide, in the market towns of Bedale, Northallerton and Topcliffe, and elsewhere. They had had several copies of it made and had gone so far as to have

geven the same to stage players who by practyce and procurement haue at the ending of their playes sunge the same as a Jygg to the great sclandall

of Michael Steel, who as a result has been brought into utter disgrace among his neighbours. Meynell and the others were content to answer with a general denial of any conspiracy to defame Steel and his supposed maidservant. But they were served with subpoenas to attend the Council of the North, whereupon tempers already frayed grew explosive.

Steel reported in a Replication, dated 25 January 1604, after the case had been taken to the Star Chamber in London, that Meynell and Bowes had threatened him outrageously and had beaten a kinsman of his. Bowes stood in William Bell's shop in Northallerton and announced his intention to give stripes to Steel if he showed his face in market there, and would moreover bring down blue-caps, 'meaning borderers or north Country men', to kill him. Meynell, for his part, attending a race meeting, was so indignant at the very sight of Todd, a relative of Steel, that he took 'a switching rodd' to him on the spot, in this public assembly, a great affront to Steel. The unhappy messenger who presented Meynell with the subpoena received hard words and harder blows in return, and a message was given to Steel which is worthy of record. Meynell would make Steel, he said, find four pairs of legs when the two principals met, a threat which Steel takes pains to interpret to the Council,

meaning as yt should seeme to make (me) Run away for fear of being killed.

And there is no doubt that is what Meynell must have meant. Meynell, indeed, flaunted his intentions publicly in North-allerton, riding up and down the town on market day, ostentatiously displaying an unseemly instrument of punishment and proclaiming his search for his enemy. Steel, by a fortunate chance, did not go to market that day and so escaped assault and battery.

Meynell rejoins, on 23 May 1604, denying his knowledge that Todd, whether he beat him or not at the horse-running, was Steel's kinsman, and other matters are also denied on terms not free from ambiguity, as usual. But he carries the war into the enemy's camp, and attacks his character. Steel, it seems, at least six months before the date of the making of the alleged libel, had turned his wife away from him to shift for herself, and in her place kept house with Frances Thornton, with whom he was actually living 'verye suspicyouslye' and in common ill fame and report. Indeed, Steel has been guilty of many evil practices, particularly against his legitimate wife, and his behaviour is not only wrong in itself but also a very bad example to his neighbours.

The case by now had been taken to the Star Chamber. In the interval the evidence of the defendants had been taken at York, before commissioners, on 10 October 1603, and it is of especial interest because we have the full facts concerning the making of the Jig, of which several accounts are given. Francis Mitchell, Meynell's servant, first at Hawnby and now at Hilton in Cleveland, aged twenty-two, tells the following story:

vpon a wednesdaie next before christmas daie last was Twelvmonth[1] one George Warde this deponent and others goinge towardes Allerton,...George Warde told this examinate that he knewe a good Jyste by a Neighboure of his Michaell Steele and his supposed maid servante, and desired this examinate to maik a songe thereof That they might bee merrie in christmas withall, and that...Warde affirmed to be trewe and that it would be iustified by his neighboures, and...Warde did then declare to this examinate the substance of the matter contained in the coppie of the Rime or songe now... showed...and thervpon this examinate by his...instruccons and at his requeste did contrive and maik the...Songe or Rime or the most parte of it....

The song was certainly about Steel, his wife, and his maid. So Ward said, and so Mitchell himself has often remarked. He makes no bones about it. Bowes corroborates the story. He himself was one of the company. Ward was a Gatenby man, Steel's nearest neighbour, and assured Mitchell that he would be greatly obliged by any poetic efforts resulting from the story he told, and would bear the brunt of any consequences. Later on, Bowes was again walking with Mitchell when he was maiking & writinge some parte of the...ryme or

[1] For the benefit of South-country readers, it might be well to interpret this complex date, given in North-country terms of reckoning. It is the Wednesday preceding Christmas Day, 1601.

verses, and hereing him reade some parte of the same, in merrie speeches,

sought to dissuade him from pursuing his muse.

Neither Bowes nor Mitchell lets it out that Meynell was one of the party on its way to Northallerton. Meynell does, however, and confirms all they say. Ward, he adds, was the servant of Sir Richard Theackston. As soon as Mitchell had written his libel, he took steps to communicate it to Steel, who threatened to beat him for it. Whereupon Meynell marched over to Skelton to his house, desiring to see him put his proposal to the test. But Steel was not at home, and Meynell left word that he would 'taik the maiking theareof vpon him, And see if (he) would beate him', a challenge which Steel was fain to evade. We may not altogether approve of Meynell, but we cannot deny him a stout heart, not only at Skelton but also at York and before the Commissioners.

The libel was copied out for various purposes. For example, Sir William Bellasis, 'long desirous of a coppie of the...Jygge', sent his man Robert Fox for one in the summer of 1602. And Ward had to have a copy. It was also published vocally with some frequency. Mitchell sang it in Meynell's house and in Bowes' house at Ellerbeck, and so did other servants of Meynell. Bowes has heard it sung in his own house by his servant Roger Bowlande and other retainers of his, also in other places and by other people. The last time he heard it was at Anthony Rokeby's house at Grimskarr. Meynell also has heard it, evidently several times and in many houses. And, what is of some significance,

about christmas last past he hard the...songe begune to be sunge by certaine players at Osmotherlie.

Their Jig had passed from the region of private amusement to that of public dramatic entertainment, for which it is evidently designed and upon which it is modelled. Meynell, however, put a stop to this performance at Osmotherly,

and bade the players leave off, for the reason that the matter
had reached the law-courts and that he was involved in
Steel's suit. At any rate, he says he stopped it. He does not
know who the players were, or at all events will not say. But
it is hardly likely that there would be two companies of
players in close touch with the local gentry, both taking
Osmotherly on their route. For Osmotherly was on the
regular track of the Egton players, the Simpsons' Company,
on the northerly leg of their tour from Whitby to the West
Riding and back, and near to Bowes' house at Ellerbeck.
There can be little doubt that the Egton players were involved in the incident referred to by Meynell and in the
interrogatory which asks whether the libel has not been
'sunge by stage players as a Jigge vpon the staige at the end
of their playe', whether a copy was not given to them for
that purpose, and whether the libellers or their agents did
not 'Call for the Jigge att the end of any play'. The Jig itself
has fortunately survived, in a copy attached to the Bill as an
exhibit and as evidence.

It is written upon a single sheet of paper, $16\frac{1}{4} \times 12\frac{1}{4}$ in.,
elaborately ruled into three columns. The second column
begins at 'To the Tune of ffortune', and the third at 'To the
Tune of ffor her Aperne'. It is evident from certain slips in
the text that it is a copy of the original, not the original itself.
But it is no less clearly a copy made for local use, and made
with some care and with some decorative intention. It was
probably the copy which Mitchell conveyed to Steel for his
edification, and Steel had it attached to his Bill of Information.

The Jig is set out, indeed, in dramatic form, with speakers'
names prefixed to their parts of the dialogue. The speeches
are mostly separated by single rules. The tunes are indicated,
dividing the whole as it were into scenes, and are enclosed
in double rules. There is a good deal here that is parallel to
the form of extant prompt copies of plays, and it is probable
that we have in this manuscript a typical example of the copy
for a stage-Jig. The whole play is sung to the specified tunes,

a change of tune signifying a new section of the action. There is no indication of any dance forming part of the perform-ance.[1] For what it is, it is not an incompetent piece of work, and has considerable sense of elementary drama, with a definite action and some interest of its own apart from its scandalous topical allusiveness.[2] It is here reproduced as it appears in the manuscript, except for the division into columns and the ruling, with the original spelling and punctuation, but correcting a few slips and deletions.

§ ii. *MICHAEL AND FRANCES*

To the tune of *ffiliday fflouts mee*

M. Come to me pritty Lasse.
 and Harken to my Plainte.
ffor since I maried was.
 I have Liued discontent.
My wife is very olde.
 I Cannot merry be.
there is nor wealth nor golde
 Can make her sweete to me:
I Lye both daie and night
 in suche a Heauye plighte.
that nothinge can delight.
 Comforte me ffauncis.[3]

F. Sweet Michaell shewe yor greefe
 vnto yor trustie ffrende.
yf I can yealde releife.
 you shall have me at Comaunde.

---

[1] The prosecution raises an interesting question concerning the addition of an 'under-song' since the death of Queen Elizabeth. This phrase appears to mean merely added stanzas, and is so understood by the witnesses, who deny any such addition.

[2] Steel accuses his tormentors of being 'common libellers'. It may be that Mitchell had some local repute as a maker. Certainly Ward goes to him as an expert for the song, furnishing the preliminary material for the requisite work of art.

[3] *Sic.*

And ffaithfull will I proue
  Soe longe as life doth last.
Doubte not my dearest Loue
  but shew yor Sorrowes past
And I will ready bee
  to ease yor maladie.
In this extremetie.
  welcome to Frauncis:

_M._   For this Kindnes of Love
      a thousand thanks to the
    yff thou wilt Constant proue
      I will disclose to thee
    the greefe and mightie paine
      I live in Howerly
    with suche a Jelous queane
      ffrowninge soe sowerly
    That livinge in this striffe
      I loose my very life
    ffye on my wicked wife
_F._   Welcome to ffrauncis.

_M._   This night yf thou Consent
      I meane so sicke to be
    My wife thou shalt acquainte
      with my Infirmitie
    And shew her in this Case
      I meane alone to lye
    And to haue thee my Lasse
      to beare me Companie
    Where we shall passe this nighte
      with greate Joye and delighte
    suspected of noe weight
_F._   Welcome to Francis.

_F._   It shall not be denyed
      to worke this pollicie
    ffarewell sweete Mr myne
      I goe with speed from thee
    vnto my Mrs then
      for to shew her this Case

M.   Adue sweete I praie,
        god guide you on the waie
    I shall praie night and daie
        ffor my sweete ffrauncys.

To the Tune of *ffortune*

Wife Come ffrauncis Come make hast and goe with me
      it is tyme to rest for suche a one as me
    my bones are olde and bloude has fledd awaie
      I marvell muche what makes my husband staie
F.   Hard happ god watt yor husband is not well
      sore sicke he lyes and willed me to tell
    He is in bed and meanes alone to lye
      and for his case woulde haue noe Companie
Wife Alac Alac woe worth this luckles night
      and fie uppon this Luckles wight
    who hath enioyed my ritches and my treasure
      and for all that in me he takes no pleasure
    whie would he refuse to lye with me his wife
      as Carefull of his health as of my life
    And would not make me privie to his greeffe
      who would haue sought to yealde him some releefe
F.   O Mrs deare lett all yor Sorrowes passe
      some Sodaine ffitt oppressed him alas
    Tomorrow I hope in god he wilbe well
      till then god Night and soe I bid farewell

To the tune of *take thy old Cloake about thee*

M.   What newes quoth he my prettie peate
      mee thinks thou lookes full merely
    How faires my wife is she in bedd
      that I may haue thy Companie
F.   Good sir yor wife is malecontent.
      but what of that it greeves not me
    what propper man would give consent
      to lye with such a drugge as shee.

M.   Come on sweete hart and doe not staie
        for sore I longe in bedd to be
    where we shall haue good sporte and plaie
        And passe this night with game and glee.

F.   Leade you the waie Ile Come a pace
        I thinke the tyme as longe as yee
    Till each the others Corps imbrace.
        Lye still old queane a poxe on the

To the Tune of *the Ladies of Essex Lamentacon*

Wife   Sighinge sore in woofull wise.
        with heauie harte and waterie eyes
    Noe rest nor quietnes Can I take
        to thinke vppon my vnkinde make
    Who hath against all lawe and righte
        fforsaken me poore seely wighte
    Allac and welladaye will I singe
        Since my Joyes they are done
    Welladay will I singe nowe

John   How noe good Cosen whatt makes you mone
        In suche a Case to be alone
    That you can take no sleepe nor rest
        but be with greeffe soe sore opprest

Wife   I feare that ffrauncis is this nighte
        possessed of my lawfull righte. alac.

John   Allthoughe I be her brother deare
        to punnishe her I will not spare
    with due desert for such an offence
        to such a Craftie wanton wenche
    Therefore make hast and doe not staie
        Come followe me I will leade the waie. Alac:

To the Tune of *ffor her Aperne*

(Frances)   What gallant hap had I
        Lustie brave lasse
    To scape soe soudenly
        from an olde dotinge asse

with my aperne with my aperne
And here I meane to hide my face
   with my white aperne
Shee was not soe secretly
   within the Chamber dore
But I stole as prively
   Into this hall flore: With my Aperne &c.
Here in this present place
   will I seeme to be
Sounde sleepinge on the grounde
   When they Come to seeke me. with my Aperne &c
Soe shall I sure bee
   ffree from all blame
And evermore henceforth
   Keepe my most honest name.

To the Tune of *the Cobler*

Wife   Come John what shall we doe
      now for to finde her
    I marvaile much in mynde
      what is become of her
    But wee will not leave it thus
      vntill we finde her
    yett I hope all is well
      since she is not yonder.
John   But look what I doe espie
      The sleepie wenche where she doth Lye
    What ffrauncis rise vp now I crie
      Come to yor Mrs quickly
Wife   Call againe Cosen John
      Call out I pray you.
John   Whatt ffrauncis are you deaffe
      Can you not heare me
M.   What stirr is this I heare
      Are you now maddinge
    Sicke men Cannott take theire rest
      for this yor gaddinge.

I heare of yor suspicious heade
   allthoughe extreamely sicke I laide
you thought that I had bene in bedd
   with this yor maiden ffrauncis
I wishe you make amendes
   for this greate Slaunder
vniustly laide vppon her
   for me you tender

John   Cosen yor ffault is greate
   therefor Crave mercie

Wife   pardon vpon my knees
   my extreame ffollye
ffor never will I till I die
   suspect my husband wrongfully
Good michaell thinke no worse on me
   but let vs end in ffreind shippe

finis

(iii) *Fool's Fortune* in Shropshire

§ i. A SHROPSHIRE HEIRESS

The story of the matrimonial adventures of Agnes Howe, which led to Chapman's play, *The Old Joiner of Aldgate*, at the Paul's theatre in London, had its parallels in the provinces, with a similar employment of the stage and drama as a move in the quarrelsome game of intrigue excited by the emergence of a marriageable heiress. In the later years of James I, such a dispute arose in the remote county of Shropshire, the records of which afford the most notable example of the provincial libel-play in its highest elaboration. Its writer hides himself from our knowledge. Nor would he, if his name were known, trouble the historian of literature, for its literary value is negligible. The actors were amateurs, and their ability unrecorded. But their exploits in the dramatic field indicate how the national passion for the play expressed itself, when stimulated by need and occasion, and with the example of the full-grown literary drama as a model, in a form that went far beyond the older, more elementary dialogue-Jig.

The aggrieved parties in this case, who took their troubles to the Court of Star Chamber in March 1622, were John Ridge, the parson of Claverly in Shropshire, some five miles east of Bridgnorth, his daughter Elizabeth and her husband William Pratt, yeoman, of Bobbington in Staffordshire, a neighbouring village. The story, as they tell it, is one of un-principled conspiracy on the part of Humfrey Elliott, a gentleman and one of Ridge's parishioners, against 'the in-nocence of the vnexperienced yeares of vnmaried damsells', to wit, Elizabeth, Ridge's only daughter. Elliott was aware that she would be endowed with all her father's estate, and therefore sought, 'out of a most Covetuse & greedie desire to gaine', to dispose of her in marriage. There were two ways of doing so. Either he might arrange for her to marry a fellow-conspirator, who would reward him for his labours. Or he might marry her himself, in which event he would pay the reward. The whole project demanded, it seems, no less than twelve conspirators, including three gentlemen, Elliott, his brother William, and Thomas Whitmore, and a group of 'laborers', with one 'spinster', Elinor Smyth, and one married woman, Margaret Soley. So they laid their plans, and in August 1619 the first step was taken. Edward Hinkes, a Claverly yeoman, was insinuated as a servant into the Vicar's house, in order that he should use his opportunities of access to Elizabeth to urge Elliott's suit upon her. If, alternatively, he found Elizabeth 'not inclinable to' Elliott, he should woo her for himself. Elizabeth, in fact, refused his overtures for Elliott. So in due course they concentrated their hopes upon Hinkes' chances, though him also she 're-solutely and scornefully denyed'. Nevertheless, in pur-suance of their plot, they thought it well to scare off all other possible suitors, and to this end they spread abroad 'slander-

ouse tales and Reproaches' against the girl, accusing her of
undue familiarity with Hinkes, and went so far as to

devulge the same in diuers scandalous and Infamous lybellus
verses Rymes plaies and enterludes,

the texts of which are then given in the Bill, with some details to follow concerning the significance of the libels, the
acting of them, and the parts taken in them by various
members of the group of conspirators. The main libel, in
the form of a play, has for its chief characters Jenny, who
stands for Elizabeth, and Jockey, who is Edward Hinkes.
Jenny's part was played by William Hardwick, whom they

did apparell & disguise...in womens apparell bolstered & set
owt in shew,

and Richard White and others acted other parts, apparelled
'in seuerall other formes and fashions of attyre', White
playing the part of Jockey. The play was performed

in the presence of a great Number of your Maiesties subiects so
assembled purposely vpon the...saboth daie to heere the same
at Claverly

and also at other places several times,

the...actors & confederats much reioysinge at the sainge actinge
plainge & Repeatinge therof.

There was moreover another

wrightinge in the nature & fforme of an Interlude or plaie in
prose,

also acted at Claverly, in which a certain John Bett, in
women's clothes, did

plaie & Represent a most Impudente bould audaciuse strumpett.

In both cases there was no manner of doubt that Elizabeth
was being pilloried.

   In spite of all these efforts to discredit her, however,
Elizabeth was shortly after married to William Pratt. The
conspirators thereupon proceeded to extremes, with the help

of reinforcements from London, whence two ruffians were recruited, along with John Gravenor, another Claverly labourer. Hinkes now took charge. Knowing that Elizabeth and her husband were due, on 14 July 1621, to be walking by night along the road leading out of Claverly towards a bridge on their way to her father's house near by, these four men lay in wait, intending to murder them. A couple of country folk courting chanced to pass along, fortunately for the Pratts, but unfortunately for themselves. William Knowles and Alice Prestwood, thus assaulted by mistake, fled back to Claverly, hotly pursued by Hinkes and his party, in such a rage and fury that Claverly folk 'were Inforced to Ryse out of theire bedds to saue them'.

Finally, a month later, the baffled conspirators had resort to one last device, seeking to prove that Elizabeth and Hinkes had entered into a contract of marriage, and that her marriage to Pratt was illegal. To this end they suborned witnesses, who swore false evidence, David Evans being bribed with the gift of a dagger, Elinor Smyth with five shillings, Richard Soley and Margaret his wife with maintenance and odd money.

Such is the story as told by Ridge and his family. It is distinctly difficult to accept it as an accurate, dispassionate or probable account of events. The plot seems to be altogether too complex, the number of conspirators seems excessive, the sequence of events illogical. It might seem, for example, that an allegation of precontract after an attempt at murder is a lamentable anticlimax. One turns with some interest to such alternative accounts of the facts as the accused parties furnish in their Answers. Edward Hinkes, indeed, puts a very different light upon the matter, shedding the colours of romance upon it. It appears that while he was a servant in the Vicar's house he naturally saw much of Elizabeth, who was only seventeen years old at his coming, and love grew between them, sealed in a contract of marriage. But her father came between the young lovers, and arranged for her to marry Pratt. Hinkes at once did what he was fully justified in doing. He put in a caveat against the marriage in the Ecclesiastical Court of Bridgnorth, in which Peculiar Claverly lay. Elizabeth's enthusiasm, however, if it ever existed, either had evaporated, or was frustrated. For she was cited to appear, twice, and failing each time to present herself was excommunicated. Late in August she countered by appealing to the Court of Arches in London, and obtained an inhibition of the cause in the Peculiar Court. So the case stands, and Hinkes proposes to pursue it, confident in his rights. He knows nothing of any reference to Elizabeth in the plays, nor who wrote them, and was no actor in them. As for bribery of witnesses, the most that can be alleged truly is that he gave small gifts to his fellow-servants in Ridge's house, giving 'davy' an old doublet and

an old hatt at on tyme and two pence at other tyme to Elenor Smyth a servant there in the same howse whoe vsed to drive the plowe and to doe other drudgery,

an interesting sidelight upon the organization of a Stuart parson's establishment.

It would appear that the case was not pressed against Elliott, who is not called upon to answer, and we may fairly take it that the facts concerning the relations between Hinkes and Elizabeth are probably truly stated by Hinkes, so long as we reserve the necessary doubts regarding the actual contract alleged by him. And now for the play. An Answer by Samuel Hill and Francis Day deals with this aspect of the Bill, and what they have to say is very perplexing to one who has read the play as it is copied into the Bill.

For the last twelve years, they say, they and other Claverly men have been acting plays annually in Claverly for the amusement of their neighbours and other spectators who came to enjoy them, during the summer time. Hill was the regular Clown or Fool in their plays. In the case in question, both Hill and Day

did act theere parts therein...Samuell actinge the parte of on

Joculus the foole or clowne therein and...ffrancis actinge therein the parte of one Loueland an vsurer and alsoe the parte of a philosopher.

The first performance of their play that year took place on a Sunday afternoon after evening prayer. Ridge himself said his office very early that day specifically in order to give time for the performance of the play. Moreover, Ridge and Elizabeth were actually present as spectators, and so was Pratt, not only at this first performance but at subsequent performances at Claverly. Indeed, Elizabeth followed the actors to see them perform at Bobbington,

at one tyme when the same play was acted by these defendants and theire fellowe actors in the towne of Boveton...true it is that at one of the tymes of actinge the same play one of theire fellowe actors called Danyell whose Sirname these defendants knowe not actinge the parte of one called Bravado in that play when he should as his parte was have said *Justics mittimus* daughter said in steade thereof Master Ridges daughter.

Hill and Day cannot understand what made Daniel take it into his head to insert this gag, but they are clear that no disparagement was intended to Elizabeth. For the rest, it is no crime to act plays, and their plays were not libellous.

It is evident that there has been some confusion. White and Hardwick, who are said to have acted the parts of Jockey and Jenny, representing Hinkes and Elizabeth, do not appear to answer. The play cited in full in the Bill does not correspond to that which Hill and Day describe, and has a different set of characters. The plot, as set forth in the Bill, with far greater possibilities of contumely, demands that

Elizabeth vnder the name of...Jenney should ffyrst Chardge... Hinkes vnder the name of Jockey that hee was father of her Child And that two others of the...actors should appersonate one of them vnder the name of ffurioso...Humfrie Ellotts, and the other vnder the name of Tumido an vnknowne Ruffian who should also Insynuate that they had abusd the Chastetie of... Elizabeth so appersonated by the name of Jenney.

The Bill, however, does not do full justice to the ingenuity and complexity of the argument and action of the play. Jenny opens the play, lamenting her solitariness. Presently Jockey arrives and is welcomed, showing equal enthusiasm himself until he becomes aware that Jenny is with child, a responsibility that he will not assume, though he cannot deny it. Jenny agrees with him upon a plot to shift the burden upon another of her lovers, of whom two are coming home from sea. She goes off in search of a Constable. Furioso and Tumido then appear and quarrel over her favours in antici-pation. They are apparently brothers, and decide to draw lots, with the help of Jockey, who is their servant. Furioso wins, but at this moment Jenny returns with a Constable and one Sturdy to help him. Encouraged by Jenny the Constable arrests both gallants. The question is which is to be held responsible. The dilemma is solved by both agreeing to abide by the decision of a Midwife who now enters with Doll her maid, bearing two children in a basket on her head. The Midwife settles the problem by presenting Tumido with the girl-baby and Furioso with the boy and promising to find them nurses. The party goes off. Jockey, who had slipped away, returns and sings a gleeful song, for the twins were his. He sings too soon, however, for the Constable, Sturdy and Doll come back to arrest him also on Doll's information. But Jockey takes to his heels and escapes.

Such is the plot of the play, a complete little farce or comic operetta, which obviously has nothing to do with the play described by Hill and Day in their Answer. It is evident, moreover, that such a plot can hardly have been concocted between Hinkes and the Elliotts, if it was meant to represent their relations with Elizabeth Ridge. For Hinkes would then be the triumphant comic hero, with the two Elliotts playing the roles of his dupes, the butts of Jockey and of the audience alike. They would, in fact, have been more likely to have joined in with Ridge as plaintiffs against Hinkes! I am unable to offer any explanation of the evident confusion, and of the discrepancies that seem to vitiate the allegations of Ridge. In all such dramatic libels, it is invariably difficult to make a case for direct topical allusion, for the play is so couched as to permit of alternative interpretations. The written form, moreover, does not always correspond to what was actually performed. And much depends upon the skill and malice of the actors. They were aware not only of the acute interest to be aroused by the topical turns which might be given to a play, but also of the need to safeguard themselves against just such penalties as those which Ridge sought to invoke upon them in this instance. I do not know whether he succeeded in obtaining satisfaction from the Court of Star Chamber. Nor do I know whether Hinkes pursued his matrimonial suit against Elizabeth. But I think it quite likely that Ridge's Star Chamber suit was a countermove to Hinkes' appeal to the Ecclesiastical Courts. I suppose it probable that Jockey and Jenny, Tumido and Furioso, and the Vicar himself, are all lying at peace together now in Claverly churchyard.

The play itself may properly be included among Jigs, however elaborate its structure. For it consists of a series of song-dialogues, set to specific tunes, as a medium for dramatic action. There is no definite indication of any dance as part of the entertainment. But it is difficult not to believe that Jockey's song of triumph, with its refrain 'But Jockey still goes free, goes free', was not in fact made the occasion for a dance of the jig type as accompaniment to it.

The text of the play is for the most part easily legible, and the parchment on which it is written well-preserved. But the latter part has suffered from fading, rubbing, and folding, and there are some lines towards the end which cannot be deciphered. The loss, however, is not serious, for enough remains to trace the action of the play. And the literary quality of the work is not such as to cause lamentation for its incompleteness. The text is written as continuous prose. I have therefore so far edited it as to restore its verse-form and to arrange it with the headings to its successive scenes.

§ ii. *FOOL'S FORTUNE*

ffooles fortune

to the tune of *A: B: C:*

Ginny: whenas I slept in fortunes lapp:
then tender in her fickell eye:
beinge kept by her from all mishap
from woe from shame from povertie:
then did my frends come in by flockes
the firste scarce gonn the second knockes:
And still they haunte mee frequently
still vowing love & Constancie
But sith the Castle of my fame:
is ransackte by eternall shame
Like sumer birdes they falsly flie:
the winters of my messerie.
wheras brave gallants for me stroue:
for euerie daie I had a loue
all winds did then blow sutors home:
when now thers none will at me come
which makes mee lyue thus in destresse
and pininge in my hevynes
& like the turtle making mone:
to liue lamente & lie alone:

Enter Jockey: to the tune of *barnaby*:

Ginney: welcome Jockey to thine owne sweetinge:
Jockey: Thanks sweete Jinney weell kise at our meetinge:
they kise

Ginney howe coudest thou this longe for goe mee:
& not once in a moneth come to me:
Jockey: it was because thou wouldst not loue mee
Ginny: Alasse sweet Jockey it was to proue yee:
Nea from a woman is noe denyall:
aske thrise at least to make a triall:
But sith constant I doe the finde:

To thee Ile be lovinge to thee Ile be kinde:
Ile loue thee not weekly noe noe nor yearly
Ile loue thee daylie Ile loue thee deerly:
Ile loue thee onlie. Ile loue thee euer
thers nothinge but death shall vs two seuer:

Jockey: who o o oo vp the Case is altered now I could not
haue a kise the last tyme I was heere vnder a spetiall
suplycavitt

Itts fit sweet Ginney thou shouldest be righted
and thye loue with loue requited
Ile loue thee lap thee and Imbrace thee
kyse thee clip thee and vnlace thee
But what ist I feele heere

ginney Alasse doe not spie it
it is thine owne picture yf that thou couldst see it:

Jockey: yf this by thy picture Ile none of thy payntinge:

Jinney: o turne againe Jockey & keepe mee from fayntinge

Jockey: Ile turne to thee ginney but alwaies provid
thou find another father this knaverie to hide

Jennye: Its honor sweet Jockey for to bee a father:

Jockey. To bee without warshipp I sure had rather:

ginney: A father hath blessings Cap Cursie and knee:

Jockey: Lett mothers then take such honors for mee:

Ginney: And doe you refuse your Jinney to marrie:

Jockey: my backe is to weeke such burthens to carrie
why should I take thee for to vndoe mee:

Jinnie: whi should you forsake mee havinge done this vnto mee:

Jockey: I did but in Jest for which I am sorrie:

Jinnie: It proued in earnest as appeares by the storrie:
which yf you refuse I must tell you
the lawes of the land they shall compell you,
for now it is gott it must haue bredinge

Jockey: yf I did finde gettinge then thou finde ffeedinge:

Jinne Thus be they servd that men doe trust:
whose words are false & deeds vniust:
whose flinty harts and Addears eares
regard not wofull womens teares
what should I doe I cannot die:
my whings are Clipt I cannot flie
& heere to liue thus in disgrace
its worse then hell or hellish place:

well sith they practisse knaverie
thers knaues abroade as well as they
and before Ile be abusd:
these knaues like knaues shall sure be vsd
The rorars that did doe this wronge:
will com from sea befort be longe:
& lett my belly be espied
A new knaues trap I will provid
To take these gallants vnder hand
as soone as they sett foote on land
for sith that Jacks proue periured men
what foole would trust his master John:

Enter ffurioso: Tumido gallents to the tune of *Jockey there man*

ffurioso.   its marvell shee is so longe
shee was vsd att becke to flie
vnlesse that shee doth come anon
I will forswere her companie:
Tumido: why braue Brother whats the matter:
that you mutter at her hast
yf theire were a reson why
I am the man that should dystaste:
You knowe the wench is myne by course
ffurioso[1]:   such courses now I must dysdaine
I must bee first & you shall staie
vntill her tayle bee coole againe
Tumido: Zoones I scorne thuse to bee vsd,
& will you offer to a ffrend,
s hart before Ile bee abused
our swords our loues and lyves shall end
ffurioso: have patience brother & though I bee
earnest bente against the game
Ile make a motion reasonably
yf that your furie like the same
wee will cast lotts who shall inioy her
no other strife weell have about her
yf that you drawe the longeste from mee
you shall haue the wench Ile goe without her:
Joc: Ile make the cutts
ffurioso: drawe firste brother for aduantadge:

[1] This speech-name is actually placed a line higher, in error.

Tum: the longest the longest Ile haue the prise:
ffur: Nea firste letts see what is my fortune:
  it fortunes that my brother lies:

  Enter Jinney: & the Connstable & sturdie

Tumido: Then loe shee comes enough for twentie
  take her take her to thy call:
Jac: this once Ile stepp before my master
  lest poore Jockey paie for all:
Jinney: hasten Constable they are runninge
  o faine they would vs overgoe
Constable: One knaue prevents anothers coning
  I scorne that they should serve mee soe
  to make such hast it doth not boote sir:
  heere I do arest you both.
ffurioso   How now sir knave & at whose suite sir
  to obey wee would be loathe:
Consta: Att her suite where you haue bine sutors
Jocy   draw master draw:
Consta: Nea hould your hands & doe not swagger:
ffurioso: out you knaues you base promooters
  knowe then gallants from a begger:
Constable   I am in office & doe knowe
  dyrectly what the lawe doth saie
  yf soe bee rich men doe offende
  as well as poore they must obey:
Tum: who is it sir knave that wee offend:
Consta: Loe heere shee comes thats your accusor:
Tum: although that wee for her did send
  wee haue noe stomacke now to vse her
Jinney: I would your stomacks had binne soe weake
  when you attempted my defame:
ffur: out thou strumpett basse & shamlesse
  wee knowe thee not nor scarce thy name
(Jinney)[1]   remember sir your former follies:
  vpon the same yor wrongd Jinney
ffur: lewd Impudent you lie you lie
  my shoulder shapd for noe such carriadge:
Constable: these words sweete sole they will not serve

  [1] Omitted in MS.

the law the law it shall inforce
to right the wronge:

ffur: prate not knaue
lest that wee turne thee to a cours[1]
ffor dost thou thinke that gentell blod
& men that bee most brauely borne:
will seeme to staine there noble race
with things that be the Contries scorne

Jinney: The tree is knowne still by his frught
strangers blush to heere you brage
it is a Coblers base Condytion
for to giue a maid the bagg:

ffur: An auntiente slander of the trade
to bee a maid is seldum seene
And of thy name I nere knew any
that could reach a leaven teene:

Jiney   A maid I was but you inticd mee
and attempted my dysgrace

ffur: Blith pockey queane didst thou not spice mee
the first tyme I sawe thy face

(*Jinney*)   ffalse mens words they are noe slander
sweet Neybour keepe them both in hould
I must home I burst in sunder
my torments they are manyfold
O my back o my bones O my head doth cleaue in twayne
I may thanke myne owne kynd harte
for procuringe all this paine:

Constable: looke to them Sturdie

Joc: its better for to bee a foole
then to bee a rich mans Child
for fooles oft tymes they have great fortunes
when the wiser are beguild
As plainly now it doth apeare
by this my luckey Jockeys case
wheras the sarvant sings the song
and the master beares the basse
harke.   harke harke:

ffur: brother sith that wee be taken
& censure most abide
be it what it will as lovinge frends

[1]   =*corse.*

　　　　our costs & Chardges weell devide:
Tum:　fair words fond fellows they may flatter
　　　　& the ffolish man beguile
　　　　but with mee hers noe such matter
　　　　I like not to Devid such spoils
　　　　the law allowes no such particion
　　　　nor ffathers more then one to bee
　　　　wherfor sweet sir as you did gett it
　　　　you shall keep it......
ffur:　vnless that thou wilt yeald
　　　　& vow to mee to keepe a part
　　　　as a parte to thee belongs
　　　　I vow to see thy faithlesse harte
Sturdy　Be quiett gent be quiett helpe master helpe:
Tum:　I scorne to take a part in paine with him
　　　　he would haue all the sport
　　　　remember that you did me wronge:
ffur:　then base false ffrend have at thy harte

　　　　　Enter the Constable　*Exit* Jockey hee creeps:
Joc:　O the Constable the Constable scape now & scape for euer
Constable:　keepe the peace or strike them downe
　　　　Ile haue noe brablinge heere beleevit
　　　　yf either offer once a blow
　　　　strike him downe that first shall giue it
　　　　whats the matter that you brable
Tum:　the matter is I wrong sustaine
ffur:　Judg you yf having sharre in pleasure
　　　　must not likwisse sharre in paine
　　　　hee had his parte with mee in pleasure
Tum:　so perhaps had many more
　　　　but you as fools doe promise maryadge
　　　　& are like to paie herefore
　　　　& I the same will witnes with you
ffur:　Ile witnes you did what you durst
Tum:　but second actions naught prevaile
　　　　but only to destroie the first

　　　　　Enter the mydwiffe & doll her maid with a maultsiue
　　　　　　　with two Children one her head
Constable:　heers comes a matron graue & learned
　　　in the art of Lechery

Lett her now end all greife between you
& sett things streight which be awrie
what saie you mother these two gallants
kyst a wench & shees with Child
now you must Judg who ought to keepe it
but lett the wench not be beguild:

Midwyfe: ffirst I would haue you for to binde them
to abide the end I make

Tum: wee both agree

Midwyfe: then doll sett downe
Ile fitt them for the wenches sake
Heers for you your Mistris token
A boie which you cannot dislike
And hers for you a bounsinge wench
O hould your hands & doe not strike:

ffur: Zoones giuest mee a foolish wench
take it back vnto the mother:

Mid: & why not you good sir I praie
goe drincke vntoot as well......
Take it take it & be thankfull
& that I may prevent your Curses
follow mee and I will shew you
where that you shall gett your nurses

Exnt: Mid: Const: sturdy: ffur: Tumido:

Doll   Its hapie that poore doll is easd of her load
&.........other waie
for it is oddes I went to looke
a needle in a load of haye
O one Jockey should haue had the wench
but sith he scaped in such sorte
the tricke is new & yf I fynde him
Jockey hee shall paie mee forte

Enter Jockey to the tune of the new masque

the proverb it proves still true for mee
wheras all doe saie its better to be
a foole then to bee a rich mans child
for fooles they have fortune the wyse are beguild
for Jockey still goes free goes free
for Jockey still goes free

wheras noe lesse then a Cuple of babes
of Jockes owne gettinge of the drabes
haue fathers.....................
.........gallants proue nurces for mee
and Jockey still goes free goes free
and Jockey still goes free
But now sith that the daunger is past
& I am free Ile haue another cast
sith I haue the...................
...................nurce againe
for Jockey still goes free goes free
for Jockey still goes free

Enter the Constable sturdy doll

Constabell   yett not so free as you supose
   you shall be a ffather in dispite of your nose
   the Child......................
   .....her & find...........gett it
Jockey   no. no. no.
Constabell   But did you not gett it
Jockey: no:
Constable   This no: no: no: it will not serve
   Although you deny the Child to deserve
   The wench...her..........to h......hers two
   ....the..........is true
   And cann you deny it
Jockey   no no no
Const   can you deny it
Jockey   no
(Constable)[1]   then what will you giue me yf I doe tell
   a tricke to defeate her this trike I can sell
   com out with your money and down with yor purse
Jockey: no: no no never the Child is at nurse
   and Jockey still goes free goes free
   & Jockey still goes free
Constable: nea yf you had hope heers one will depose
   shee said you inforced her her credit to loose
   its death by the law & hange thou shalt
   & art thou not guilty of this fault
   confesse confesse

[1] Omitted in MS.

Jockey   & be hanged & be hanged
  confesse & be hanged
  .... of this crime:
  shee should have confesd it before this time:
  the daunger is past:
Const: first gett release
  com com I must have you to a Justice of peace
  ffor Jockey must not goe free goe free
  for Jockey must not goe free:
Jockey harke first Mr Constable a worde in your eare
  nea come further of they ought not to heare
  this all that I saie to him thats in bannds
  one paire of heeles is worth two payre of hands:
Const: O hould the theiffe hees gone
  O hould the theiffe hees gone

Chapter IV

THE MAY GAME

(i) *The May Game*

The May Game does not lend itself readily to historical
treatment. As far back as it can be traced it has already become intertwined and confused with other forms of ancient
popular festivity, such as the Morris Dance. The Queen of
the May herself is of a very respectable antiquity, as an in-
stitution, so antique indeed that, in the absence of facts, a
vacuum which human nature abhors, theories have supplied
an imaginative history of May Games and the like which is
of the kind favoured by anthropologists. The May Game is
held to be a form of rite arising out of the Fertility Cult. Its
personages are vegetation deities or priests. The Maypole
is a sacred tree, and the Game a kind of sacrifice. This kind
of explanation takes also within its ambit the Morris Dance,
the Sword Dance, St George and the Dragon, and Robin
Hood and his merry men. In the meantime we have little
documentary knowledge such as would enable us to reconstruct the actual development through the centuries of
this form of merrymaking, still less enough to trace it back
to the prehistoric solemnities from which it is held to have
degenerated into mirth. The play-instinct, after all, may well
have actuated the earliest of men even before he developed
the most primitive of religious myths, much less the highly
elaborate concepts and rites of the Fertility Cult. The word
'primitive', indeed, is too often used to disguise the real
complexity of ideas and customs which can only have arisen
in highly developed communities. What we actually know
for a fact concerning the basic elements of the May Game

needs no interpretation other than as organized play of an intelligible kind. There is something to be said for the child's point of view which Tennyson set forth in a pair of poems which were once favourably known to the children of a less anthropological England.

Tennyson's *May Queen* and *New Year's Eve* are quite unbiased. He had merely seen and taken part in May Games such as Lincolnshire had practised and enjoyed for many centuries. Consequently he has the root of the matter in his poems. In them you find May Day, a Maypole, a May Queen, garlands, and dancing round the pole on a village green. Effie's little friend, on her day of glory, had no notion that she was placating any hostile deity, or helping the farmer to a bumper crop. It was May Day, the sun was out again and strong, the May blossom was on the hedgerows, the air was scented with it. The long winter, whose cruel oppressiveness only recent times have lightened for mankind, was well past and over. And the birds were singing again. Why should not village folk go out in the fresh morning and gather the May, symbol of all this renewed brightness, choose one of themselves to preside over their festivities, garland her, enthrone her, and dance round her with song and mirth? It all seems a very likely thing to occur to them, the more likely indeed, the more primitive they were.

It has often occurred to me that another ancient game, if we may not be allowed to accept it as mere play, might be made susceptible of a more learned explanation. Originally it was, of course, a winter game, as it still is, and in the dark backward and abyss of time primitive man, so primitive yet so complex, made an image of the world and, longing for summer, sought to hasten the revolution of the seasons by propelling his toy earth severely round a field. It is an attractive theory. It explains the origin of football, and it proves that primitive man knew the world to be round. But the facts show that in truth an ancient game has had symbolic and ritual accretions added to it. In various parts of England popular anthropology has associated it with ancient battles, commemorated by a general *mêlée* through the streets, as in Chester-le-Street with its Up-streeters and Down-streeters, contumeliously kicking throughout the strenuous day the symbolical head of a slain Danish enemy, according to a firm traditional belief. Whether the Dane was a fact or not, this accretion is a fact. So here also we are dealing with facts. Tennyson, it will be observed, introduces a Robin, the May Queen's wooer. And this is truly scientific, for it is based on a fact. Poets generally do deal with facts, of one kind or another. The essential features of the old May Game were few in number. On May Day the people celebrated the return of summer. They appointed rulers of their merriments, after the organizing fashion of the English, any two or three of whom, left alone on a desert island, would soon found some kind of a club. So we have a Lord and Lady of the May who preside. Having a Lord and Lady, a King and Queen, they must be entertained. So the presence of temporary royalty becomes a pretext for the exhibition of such shows as local folk can manage, in the shape of local pastimes practised and devised for such a great occasion, with dancing, singing, speeches, processions in disguise. So necessarily there must be some one to introduce and direct the shows. The Presenter is essential to the occasion. As it was desirable to have some mirth in the proceedings, and as the Presenter or Leader ought to be a man of ready wit, able to improvise, the local humorist was obviously the proper person. Moreover, Kings took pleasure in jesters, and allowed them privileges and liberties. So the Presenter was normally in the character of a Fool, and with him went inevitably other grotesque characters in ancient favour, such as the Hobby-Horse in particular.

The May Game, it would seem, has developed in the direction of the Masque in its simplest form, a Disguising, the purpose of which is to visit a great person with some ceremony, in order to pay homage. It is transferred to the open fields. The people for once make their own Lord and Lady, and two of their own folk rise each year to royal dignity for a day. But the ceremony is the same. It is a parallel, if parallels must be sought, to the Boy Bishop game, or to the Saturnalia. By the time we have historic records of any one set of May Games, we find greater complexity than this, of course. We may find, for example, that in place of the Lord and Lady we have Robin Hood and Maid Marian. This for two reasons. First, Robin stood for the assertion of an Englishman's notion of freedom from tyranny, and so could well take the May Lord's place. And secondly, the Robin Hood story was a frequent theme of popular dramatic art, and doubtless such a play was often acted at the May Games. Why not make Robin and Marian preside? Besides, a popular kind of lyric song in dialogue with dancing dealt with the loves of a shepherd and shepherdess. What name more frequent in such lyrics than Robin, the Robin of Henryson's *Robin and Makyn* and a hundred others?

This simple instance may serve to show the infinite possibilities of variations in the development of the May Game. So it is, obviously, with the constituent parts of the ceremony in general. There are the invariable features of the homage and the garlanding, as also of the dancing round the Maypole. But the shows presented depend upon the tastes and the resources of the community.

A Marprelate tract, *Hay any Work for Cooper*, relates how a clergyman of Halstead, Glibbery, so far derogated from his cloth as to take the part of the Fool in a May Game, in the train of a Summer Lord, the shows being a Morris Dance and a play of Robin Hood. The Morris Dance was evidently practically an invariable part of the shows, as one might expect from its wide popularity as a folk dance in village life. The Morris Dance, indeed, in its later developments, has added to itself most of the features of the specific summer May Game, such as the Lord and Lady and the Fool, and even the Robin Hood element, all very confusing to historians of Folk Play.

Nashe, in his *Praise of the Red Herring*, seems to make no distinction between a May Game and a Morris Dance. But in his *Return of Pasquil* (1589) the Morris is definitely an element within the May Game which he imagines as furnishing parts for his Puritan enemies. The May Game of Martinism is

very defflie set out, with Pompes, Pagents, motions, Maskes, Scutchions, Impreases, straunge trickes and deuises.

'Penry the welchman' is to be 'foregallant' or captain of the Morris. Martin Marprelate himself is to be Maid Marian

trimlie drest vppe in a cast Gowne, and a Kercher of Dame Lawsons, his face handsomlie muffled with a Diaper-napkin to couer his beard, and a great Nosegay in his hande, of the principalest flowers I could gather out of all hys works.

Wiggenton is to be Jack Pudding or Fool, courting Maid Marian. Paget is to be the whiffler, clearing the way with two great clubs. And the keeper of the stocks of the Bridewell at Canterbury is to follow behind the procession, with a purse to gather offerings.

Let us turn back to a performance of the May Game in London in 1552, as it is recorded in Machyn's *Diary*:

The xxvj day of May came in to Fanchurch parryche a goodly may poll as youe have seen. It was pentyd whyt and gren, and ther the men and women did wher abowt ther neke baldrykes of white and gren, the gyant, the mores-danse, and the...had a castylle in the myd with pensels, and the...plasys of sylke and gylded; and the sam day the lord mayre by conselle causyd yt to be taken done and broken.

This was under Edward VI, and the Lord Mayor no doubt feared the anger of the iconoclast Reformer Somerset. But with Queen Mary and with the return of Catholicism, which approved of Maypoles, came the heyday of the May Game in London. In 1555 the St Martin's Game boasted a giant, hobby-horses, Morris Dance, drums and guns; and at West-minster all these shows, and the Lord and Lady of the May riding gorgeously to boot, with devils and minstrels and bagpipes and viols.

So also in 1559 under Elizabeth, at St John Zachary's, there rode in procession the Nine Worthies, St George and the Dragon, Morris Dancers, and Robin Hood with all his meinie, and on 25 June the whole set of shows went to Greenwich to perform before the Queen and the Council. Such was the May Game in its most elaborate form, each show being dramatic as well as processional pageantry, with speech, dialogue, song and dance.

No provincial town, of course, had the resources in men and money that a great London parish had. But they were capable of no mean efforts, and civic pride was strong then as now in the provinces as well as in London. The town of Wells furnishes some of the earliest records of May Games, and they continued to be practised there as elsewhere, in spite of Puritan attempts to put them down throughout the country. The time had not yet come to write the epitaph of the hobby-horse which Hamlet reports:

> For O! for, O! the hobby-horse is forgot.

The Puritan Stubbes found ample material in his own day for his attacks upon May Games in his *Anatomy of Abuses*, in 1583. Indeed, some years after the printing of Shakespeare's great play, the town of Wells at least was still rejoicing in hobby-horses and other ancient delights.

(ii) *The Wells May Game*

§ i. REVELS IN WELLS

It is a happy chance that the records of the Court of Star Chamber preserve for us the fullest account, in great detail, of a very elaborate May Game organized at Wells in the summer of 1607. There were elements in these festivities which were brought to the notice of the Lord Chief Justice, sitting in Assize at Taunton, at which he was 'greatly offended', and in due course came to the ear of the Chancellor, Lord Ellesmere, who went into the matter very closely himself. In the Bridgewater manuscripts, now in the Huntington library in California, we have his own minutes on the matter supplementing the Star Chamber records. Truly, Wells was in the news for a year or two, by virtue of keeping up old customs.

There was a reason why the May Game of that year was especially elaborate at Wells. The inhabitants of the parish of St Cuthbert in the town were proud of their ancient church. Now in 1607 they found it to be in sore need of repair. One of their bells was broken; another needed to be recast; and the steeple was falling down. The ordinary parish levies could not meet the case. They therefore resolved to hold a great Church Ale, a time-honoured way of raising money in festive and painless fashion, and heartily disapproved by Puritan feeling, which was opposed to festivity in general, and apt to confuse virtue with painfulness. Stubbes is very bitter about Church Ales, in which, as he sees it, 'dronken Bacchus bears swaie'. But this, if not without foundation, was a jaundiced view of the matter, which Sir Toby corrects in answer to Malvolio, with direct reference, I think, to these useful jollifications.

What, because thou art virtuous shall there be no more cakes and ale?

One of the Wells men involved in the case, Oliver Martin, a labourer, tells how he and some others, at the time of the May Game, came back to Wells

from an ale which was made at a poore weivers house at Corscomb to help him,

about six o'clock in the evening, and all were sufficiently free from the sway of Bacchus to perform their part in the Morris Dance immediately on their arrival.

The usual thing, according to Stubbes, was for the church-wardens to invest the church stock or funds in malt to be made into ale, which was then sold at a profit. But on this occasion at Wells it seems clear that a communal feast was organized, the parishioners contributing money and provisions. And the whole parish went to drink and have supper at the Church House, where the feast was held, paying for their food and drink, and raising after this fashion a considerable sum of money, a total of no less than forty-five pounds, in a parish in which the total parish levy for the year amounted only to £18. The Dean of Wells himself, Dr Benjamin Heydon, gave his full consent and approval, and with it the use of the Church House for the purpose. The May Games were organized to add to the distinction of the occasion, and to advertise the Church Ale by a variety of shows in procession, whereby men from other parishes and from the villages near Wells would be attracted and contribute to the success of the venture. The Mayor of Wells and his brethren, the chief men of the city, went in procession to sup at the Church House. Nothing, it would seem, could mar the harmony of the proceedings, so universally approved for so good an end, and redounding to the credit and fame of Wells, that city which not only possessed a Cathedral and Bishop, or at least half a Bishop, shared with Bath, but boasted also of a cor-poration and charter granted by Henry VIII, with its own liberties and everything fine about it.

But Wells, and the parish of St Cuthbert's, were reckoning without John Hole. John Hole was a clothier in Wells, and a great benefactor to Wells after his fashion, as a later Mayor of Wells, John Ashe, bears witness. For twenty years he has employed as many as three or four hundred persons, in and about Wells, spinning and making baize cloth and knitting stockings and fustians and so forth. There have been fewer beggars in Wells since he came. And he was particularly valuable to the city, because most of the persons he set to work were children, who otherwise would have been a burden upon their parents or upon the parish. But he was not a popular person in Wells, not even with the children, who sang a libel upon Hole with gusto. He had actually been 'disburgessed' or disfranchised by the efforts of his fellow-citizens. He had been accused before the Bishop of adultery with one Mrs Yard. And when Edmond White, a prominent figure in these affairs, was Constable, he took his chance to put Hole in prison for visiting London during a plague season there, thus risking the health of Wells. And now Hole refused to have anything to do with the great Church Ale. Moreover he had three friends, tradesmen like himself, who were equally out of sympathy with the common effort.

And now the whirligig of time had made Hole Constable, with no small authority, during the period of the festivities. Moreover, it is a matter of common agreement, even among neutral opinion, that he was a very strict Constable, and indeed officious in the performance of his duty, especially concerning all civic pastimes, and a rigid Sabbatarian. 'It was a hard matter', it was generally felt, 'when one man shoulde stand against the Maior and masters of the whole Towne, and also refuse to goe to the Church Alle with his neighbors.' So William Tiderlegh reports, a witness on behalf of Hole, and a Judas to the other party, for he betrayed a copy of a certain libel to Hole and to the Star Chamber in due course. And Tiderlegh narrates a sample of Hole's part in the festivities. On 17 May 1607, Tiderlegh was standing at the High Cross in Wells. There he saw Hole busy at the Cross, charging the substantial watch, after the fashion of Dogberry in *Much Ado about Nothing*. As he was thus busied, there came round the Cross through the street

trooping together about some 30, or 40, men in marshall manner with weapons, & a drum and Trumpetts sounding, and Emongest that company was one Edward Cary whome they termed Captayne Cary.

Hole marched up to Cary, halting the procession of Morris men, and ordered them to depart each man to his lodging.

Cary answered, very civilly and using no ill words, that they were precisely proceeding to their lodgings. So Hole, non-plussed, withdrew to his Watch. The procession set forth again, and in a moment the trumpets were once more in full blast as they passed away through the market-place.

I think I hear a snatch of the dialogue which ensued when Hole rejoined his fellows of the Watch:

Watch How, if 'a will not stand?

Dogberry Why then, take no note of him, but let him go; and presently call the rest of the watch together, and thank God you are rid of a knave.

Verges If he will not stand when he is bidden, he is none of the prince's subjects.

Dogberry Indeed, the watch ought to offend no man, and it is an offence to stay a man against his will.

Hole had taken occasion more than once to confront various other processions during May and June of this year, halting them while he, supported by his Watch, read to them a pro-clamation against riots, and ordered them to disperse. But in vain. And he had then also, 'by the authority and duty of his place', reproved them severely, equally in vain. All he achieved was to lend strength to that malice against him of which he complained later in high places.

Hole's friends were less prominent in the opposition, of course. But two of them had been Constables too, and evidently of the same sort. There was John Yard, a haber-dasher of Wells, a man of fifty-six years of age, Humphrey Palmer, a grocer, aged forty-eight, and Hugh Mead, a pew-terer, aged thirty-five. And there was Mrs Yard, concerning whom Hole had come into scandalous question. Mrs Yard was evidently a difficult and censorious woman of rigidly Puritan views. She disapproved, for example, of Maypoles, especially of that Maypole which this year had been set up between the market-place and the church of St Cuthbert in Wells. Like many another of her way of thinking, she had been led to esteem of Maypoles as heathen idols set up for

pagan worship, and applied to them the Biblical image of
the golden calf erected by the erring children of Israel, before
which they ate and drank and rose up to play and dance.
Indeed she spoke of it daily as the 'painted calf'. As she lived
in a house on the market-place, she could not go to church
without passing the abhorred thing. So in her zeal she in-
augurated a holy strike, and refused to go to church so long
as it stood there. To the humorists of Wells this was an
opportunity not to be missed. For here we have the explanation of one of the pageants of the May Game which
at first might well have seemed inexplicable.

William Peters rode through the town exhibiting a board
on which was painted a 'sparked calf' or 'painted calf',
painted in red and white spots like the Maypole itself. Peters
was clad in skins like a Satyr, neatly combining calfdom and
paganry, and went about accompanied by Morris Dancers,
with guns, swords and drums. The party, of course, took
occasion to make a halt at Mrs Yard's door, Peters bawling
out 'ba, ba, like a calf'! After carrying the calf in procession,
the gunners shot off at it, pretending to kill it, in order that
Mrs Yard might feel free once more to go to church. A
retort courteous.

But I wonder what the anthropologists would have made
of the 'Sparked Calf' in folk play, if Mr Tiderlegh had not
reported Mrs Yard's caprice. Nothing less than a ritual blood-
offering, I am sure, and a dread memory of human, or at least
animal, sacrifice to the fertility shrine. As for Peters' disguise
in skins, it might of course have been otherwise conceived
by the Wells men: possibly their notion of primitive man
as applied to the children of Israel during the Exodus.

The rhymed history of the Wells May Game pageants,
which William Gamage wrote to his own undoing, shows
how all the most popular features of folk play were gathered
together in notable procession. The Lord of the May with
his courtiers led the way, followed by the Morris Dancers
under their Captain, Edward Cary, armed with swords,

pikes and muskets. Next came the Pinner of Wakefield and his troop, 'singing a song of Wakefilde green', and after him Robin Hood and his merry men with bows and arrows. The Sparked Calf followed, and then St George and his knights, attended by Irish footmen, and the Dragon. After them came the two Pace Eggers, carrying an egg upon a crossed staff. Then old Mother Bunch followed, sitting on a wheelbarrow making black puddings as she went. After her came the pageant of Diana and Acteon, Acteon walking in a deer's hide and horns, and Diana in triumph with six nymphs in a coach. Next came that old favourite of the Miracle plays, Noah carried on the shoulders of six men, busy building his ark. A Giant and Giantess followed, and after them an Oriental pageant of the Soldan of Egypt and his Queen riding on horses, preceded by two knights and followed by eight Irish footmen. (The Soldan of Egypt ought to have followed St George, for it is in the story of St George how he rescued the King of Egypt's daughter Sabra.) Next came the pageant of the silver plate of the city of Wells, carried by eight citizens in lawn. And finally the procession ended with the main pretext for all this pageantry, three hundred dishes of meat carried ceremoniously on its way to the Church House, to be eaten with the Church Ale already brewed and waiting there for the citizens to partake in their piously festive zeal.

There was surely no harm in all this, and nothing remotely libellous, except the Sparked Calf. And it was a genuinely communal effort. Each street devised and carried out its own pageant, and the procession had its contingents from the High Street, from Southover Street, and from Chamberlain Street, and we have a picture drawn for us of the good wives and their families busy each in their garden behind their house working on the preparation and decoration of their pageants and the disguising of their menfolk for the show. And Wells was sufficient unto itself. If a painter was needed to paint a Sparked Calf or other pictures, they knew where to find one, and Edward Cary sought out Walter Smyth,

a painter by trade, who had all the material by him, wooden
boards and paint and brushes, and his own hands and eyes,
ready to tackle a sign for an inn or anything else that a man
might do. For these were days when England was full of
craftsmen, and the word art had quite a different meaning
from today. And if a man wanted a song, in the main he set
about singing himself, except on special occasions.

Wells had a cathedral too, with notable resources. The
choristers of Wells played no small part in the pageantry,
and brought their church vestments with them. So the
heathen goddess Diana was fitly represented by a Wells
chorister, 'most sumptuous and fayre', driving in a coach,
and was hemmed in by other nymphs of the choir, whose
names are given, clad in white surplices, singing hymns
and anthems drawn from part of the Psalms of the Prophet
David. All this by the efforts of Chamberlain Street.

The highest civic authorities patronized Diana and the
show generally, for the Mayor himself and the principal
citizens of Wells walked in procession heralding the goddess
in her coach, on their way to the Church Ale in the Church
House. A certain Vertue Hunt, a Wells man, later on got
into trouble for saying that the supporters of the Games 'had
the love of the whole Towne of Wells excepte of the Tribe
of Manie Asses, thereby abusing scripture', a variation of
the Just-Asses quip of some Stratford humorists.[1] I find no
mention of the local rector or clergymen, but there is no
manner of doubt that Dr Benjamin Heydon, Dean of Wells,
had given his blessing, or at least his sanction, to these sports.

So had Mr William Evans, Master of the Cathedral
School of Wells since about 1587, who was active in their
organization. Indeed, Evans was responsible for an addition
to the festivities, which is of some interest. There was a
certain John Tanner or Attwell, who was a Proctor in the
Bishop's Court of Wells, and also, according to Evans,

a person of an humeros & manie tymes of an idle & vaine dis-

---

[1] See below, p. 195.

posicion desiros to make himself & his conceited bearinge knowne both in open merriments & private places.

Wherefore Evans and other worshipful persons went to Attwell, and

did tell the said Attwell that he must doe somethinge by way of [oration] a Speech...at yt tyme to make known his learninge & to gett Creditt & reputacion therby...or otherwise he should much obscure his learned parts...the which was spoken onelie in iest & merrie sporte & to no other end or purpose respecting onely the humeros [& idle] inclinacion of Attwell vppon which speeches...Attwell saied that he would presently goe home & drawe an oration in the comendacion of himself & of learninge.

So Attwell departed on his task, and in due course he wrote his oration in Latin, and showed it to Evans and other learned masters of the School,

perswading himself that he had done absolutelie well therein.

In the end he appeared, disguised in a velvet coat and a velvet hat 'or square corner Cappe like a Bishops hatt or Capp', ready to deliver his speech in the precincts of the Cathedral, in his 'fantasticke vainglorious humor', as Evans put it. But Evans was taking no risk of offending the chief potentate in Wells, and kept the speech, which Attwell had handed over to him for correction of his Latinity, so that Attwell had perforce to remain dumb, and in the end passed it over to the Bishop for inspection. Shortly afterwards the Bishop died, but that was a mere coincidence. The famous oration was an exhibit in the case, but, alas, is not preserved among the documents. Tiderlegh tells us that Attwell's plan was to deliver his speech at the High Cross in Wells, sitting on an ass. I imagine that Evans had spoiled an excellent piece of fun at Attwell's expense. And I further imagine that, if Evans was no bad model for Holofernes, Attwell sounds as if he was own cousin to Don Armado:

Devise, wit; write, pen, for I am for whole volumes in folio.

I have little doubt that Attwell 'drew out the thread of his

verbosity finer than the staple of his argument', and that
Evans moreover would have ample opportunity to 'smell
false Latin'. It is a great pity this oration is lost to humanity.

The pageant of St George and the Dragon was evidently
carried out with some realism. St George rode on horseback, in armour, with sword and spear. The Dragon was no
real dragon, but

the Counterfecte of a dragon with a man within him that carryed
the same & they boath represented or Acted the fighte betweene
the dragon & St George.

The Dragon, it appears, roamed the streets, and lay in wait
at a street corner in the evening to rush out and terrify the
revellers returning from the Church Ale. Whereupon
St George slew him once more. St George, I may add,
emulating Bottom, and not wishing to frighten the ladies,
was not really St George, but one Davy Trymm.

I will only add, concerning these innocent amusements,
that there was also a Queen of the May, who was dressed
up by Mrs Thomasine White on Ascension Day, along with
other little maids, her attendants, but who does not seem to
have played much part in the ceremonies, and was evidently
outshone by Maid Marian.

But it will be reasonably clear, from this prevailing in-
nocence, that the whole story cannot yet have been told.
The rhymed description of the May Game made by William
Gamage was written by him about two months after these
shows, and was written in the Bailiff's prison in Wells,
where he had other company drawn also from the Wells
May men. He was, I fear, as impenitent as Shakespeare's
Barnadine. For he sang his verses to his fellow-prisoners,
and thus helped the time to pass with renewed mirth. And
when he finally fetched up in Star Chamber, and was
examined before that high court in 1608, he refused flatly
to sign his deposition and nonplussed the Court. It took
them three days to get his signature. I wonder what led him

to obey in the end. There may have been inducements. The
Council had had some practice on Guy Fawkes not so very
long before.

The later stanzas of Gamage's song explain why the matter
passed beyond any mere accusation of profaning the Sabbath.
The early part of May was taken up with the May Games
which I have described, and with the Church Ale. But the
want of sympathy shown by Hole and his friends, and Hole's
active interference, in the exercise of his authority as Constable, demanded comment and redress. This was duly provided in later shows organized at Whitsuntide and continued
for some time, shows in which, as the Lord Chancellor was
led to note, Hole and other tradesmen were deciphered and
listed by their persons and trades. They are fully described
for us, and there is no manner of doubt that the accusation
was justified. A procession rode several times through
Wells, consisting of a group of grotesques. Mathew Lan-
caster, a husbandman, rode, disguised in women's apparel,
in a red petticoat, kerchief and muffler, like a spinster, holding
a spinning wheel in one hand and a distaff in the other with
worsted wool, turning the wheel as he rode, thus caricaturing
Hole, a clothier and spinner of worsted hose. Thomas Byson,
a lead miner, rode with a brush in one hand and a hat in the
other, and with three other old hats and a very old cap hanging at this girdle, and disguised 'in a grey beard, and flaxen
heare abowte his head', provided for him by the Bishop's
Palace,

crieinge as he so rod that he had as good hatts to sell as any
Mr Yard had in his shopp thereby vnlawfully representinge John
Yard of the same toune of Wells Habberdasher.

So John Smith portrayed Hugh Mead, deriding him, with
a plank athwart his horse, with a pewter pot, a skimmer, and
a hammer, with which he made a great din. For Mead was
a pewterer. And James Lidyard and Gamage rode face to
face on one horse,

with a paire of scales and an old frayle with graynes & other trashe in that which they flounge about in mens necks & faces saieinge aloud that Humfrey Palmer had noe such reasons[1] in his shop as they had.

Finally Robert Attwell and one Torre or Tarre rode, also both on one horse and face to face, Tarre like a Usurer with two bags full of counters, and Attwell with a small desk, pen, ink and paper, like a scrivener. There was no question of the directness of this assault, and Hole took action, bringing the performers before the Mayor's Court. But Alexander Towse was Mayor still, and he took the matter lightly. Encouraged by this, Gamage set to work upon his masterpiece, the famous Holing Game, which made John Hole a byword throughout the county. Gamage went off to see the painter again, and Walter Smyth, having agreed on his price, two shillings, carried out his instructions. Upon one board, a yard square, he painted a portrait of a woman, with a hat in one hand and a brush in the other, said later to resemble Mrs Yard, and on either side of her two men, as near as he could get to John Hole and Hugh Mead. Even the superior Mr Tiderlegh, who was a cultured person and taught Mr Evans' daughter to play the lute, agreed that Smyth's efforts

in some sorte after that grosse manner of payntinge seemed to resemble the Complainant Heugh Mead and John Yards Wiffe.

The work seems to have been highly satisfactory, in fact, for the organizers actually paid Smyth threepence above the agreed price. Under the feet of these portraits Gamage next ordered Smyth to cut nine round holes the size of a ball or bowl. Then a second board was nailed at right angles, a yard long and half a yard broad,

which serued as an vnder board or table for a ball to be trundled & tumbled vp vnto anie of the...holes.

Armed with this decorative portable game of Nine Holes Gamage only needed a horse and some bowls to add one

[1] =*raisins*.

more spectacle to the gaieties of Wells. And on 25 June he was duly to be seen on the streets in triumphant procession on horseback, practising his game and

cryeinge with a loud voyce so as manie people might heare him he holes it for a crowne & then presently it was answered by some other of that confederacye standinge by...appointed for that purpose he holes yt not for a Crowne within a yard meaninge and nameinge...John Hole by alludinge to his name.

There was also some esoteric significance in the words 'yard' and 'crown', for Mr Yard 'dwelleth at the sign of the Crowne' in Wells. Two other horsemen rode with him. On his left rode one displaying a 'pair of cards' and a 'noddie[1] board', recalling Hole's inconvenient arrest of certain minstrels for playing cards on Sunday while waiting to make music for the revels. And on his left our friend the scrivener again, to whom Gamage would cry

sett yt downe Notarye that holeinge is against the kinges proclamacion,

a manifest ridiculing of Hole's attempt to enforce the king's edict against games and riots on Sundays.

All this additional information explains a little scene which took place at the Deanery of Wells one day. James Bourne, one of the Dean's servants, tells how he was with the Dean in his parlour when sounds of prolonged and unseemly laughter were heard from the adjoining room. The Dean sent Bourne to enquire. A copy of Gamage's poem was in course of being read aloud by Henry Downton, the Dean's Clerk, to a collection of ladies, including Mrs Heydon, the Dean's wife, to whom it had come through her maidservant, Alice Croker, who was sharing in the mirth. Coming from the Dean, Bourne's presence abashed Downton. But Mrs White urged him to continue, and broke out into violent objurgations against Hole, raising her voice to such a pitch that at last

the deane himselfe came forth to pacifie her.

[1] An old form of cribbage.

And the copy which so vastly amused the Dean's household was in Gamage's own hand, and is among the archives of this case, marked *A*.

But bishops are not always of one mind with their deans, and the Bishop of Bath and Wells took a hand in the matter, with a preliminary summons of the malefactors to an examination. And at the Summer Assizes held at Taunton the Lord Chief Justice, Sir Thomas Fleming, and the Chief Baron of the Exchequer, Sir Laurence Tanfield, took a serious view of the offence. Nor was Gamage's the only libel. There was a rival poet, William Williams, alias Morgan, of a higher social position, who brought the quarrel into even more controversial ground, revived the ancient accusations of immorality against his enemies, and confounded them in one common sink of iniquity and vice with Puritanism in general. But Williams was a versifier of very different calibre from Gamage, who was after all only a shoemaker's apprentice. Williams was evidently a man of some learning and culture, and a student of the latest fashion in London satire. His libellous satire is indeed of marked literary quality, and deserves the title he gave it, *The Quintessence of Witt*. It might well, in fact, stand up to comparison with the work of any Elizabethan or Jacobean satirist except perhaps Donne or Ben Jonson. Hole was quite clear about the direction of Williams' poetic bolts, and complained that he was aimed at and referred to when Williams wrote

> Shall every Rascole, and vile Jobbernole,
> A Cytties quintessence of wytt controle?

It was rather spiteful of Williams, however, to revive memories of Marlowe's *Tamburlaine* to fling in their teeth, and to address Hole and his party in ancient dramatic verse:

> What holloe hoo, ye pampred Asyian Jades,
> must men of note and worth be your Comrades?

But it is a gratifying tribute to the undying fame of Shakespeare's great contemporary throughout the country. No wonder Tiderlegh found Williams something of an actor, when he once repeated memoriter to him Gamage's poem

which speech he deliuered with the action of his foote and hand, much like a player, which moved this deponent to thinke that the said verses had been a parte of some play.

Williams had evidently studied, as a spectator at least, in the great school of drama at London.

It was perhaps rather the pride of Wells in her *magnum opus* than any desire to spread a libel that nearly brought Gamage's verses into the category of official literature. For Edmond White, one of the ringleaders in all these affairs, conceived the notion of having them sent up to London to be printed and published. His servant Hitchcoxe was charged to find a messenger who should undertake the long journey and seek out in London a young Wells man in the printing trade there, John Budge, of St Gregory's. Budge eventually told how Thomas Haggett came into his shop and showed him the poem, asking him to arrange to have it printed, and assuring him that it recorded all the noteworthy recent festivities in Wells. There was, of course, an apparent initial advantage in approaching a fellow-townsman in Budge, but it was to prove an error of tactics. For when Budge read the verses his local knowledge made him pause,

thinckinge the same to contayne slaunderouse matter against particular persons.

Surely, he asked Haggett, stanzas 33 and 34 refer pointedly to the Constable Hole, and Haggett agreed. And there were other references to people whom Budge recognized. So in the end, Budge, a wary printer,

refused to satisfye his requeste, and soe they parted.

The Lord Chancellor's notes summarize the various ways in which the libel was published. Gamage wrote it and read it out in prison, in inns and in private houses. Thomasine White set it forth in the Dean's house, Edmond White and John Hodges in a barber's shop, Stephen Milward at a later

PLATE IV

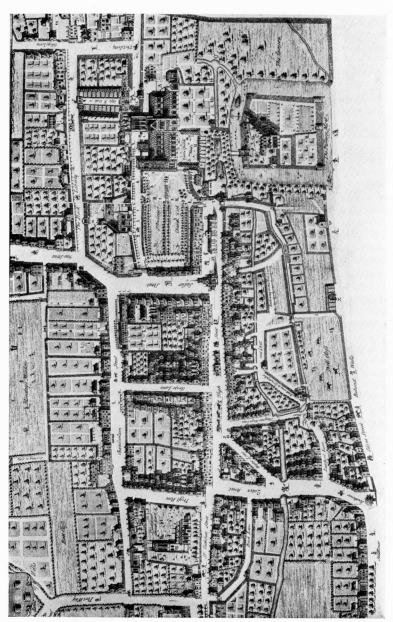

From a plan of the City of Wells by W. Sims, engraved by W. H. Toms, 1735

Church Ale, and finally Haggett attempted to have it printed. Had Budge been less cautious, or less well-informed, the story of the Wells sports might have been distributed as a broadsheet ballad throughout England in the packs of many an Autolycus, to the greater glory of Wells. And it would certainly have sold like hot cakes all over the West Country. It must have been a temptation to Budge, all the same.

The men of Wells probably saw no great harm even in the less innocent aspects of their mirth. But the Lord Chief Justice at the Taunton Assizes delivered a very severe allocution to the offenders. He went no further than this, however, and was content to bind them over. Hole was by no means satisfied, and took the matter to Star Chamber, demanding condign punishment, in proceedings which furnish us with all our information. The Court and the Chancellor took the matter seriously. Local disturbances were dangerous to the commonwealth; the times were perilous; and there were commotions in Northamptonshire which had to be borne in mind, as Lord Ellesmere notes.

The outcome of the whole business is unknown. All I can add is that by 1609 powerful protection was invoked on behalf of some of the defendants. The Earl of Hertford wrote a letter praying the Lord Chancellor to show favour to them. It was bound to be a question, on such premises, whether lenity should not be practised and so bring peace of mind both to the King's city of Wells and to the King's friend the Earl of Hertford.

I have given here versions of the literary documents in the case from the original Bill, with variants from other copies among the records. The variants show what strange things can happen in the transmission of Elizabethan copy, and have therefore their humble textual interest. The satirist Williams, when examined upon the secret significance of *Campant* in his 'epigram', poked fun at the Bill distorting the true reading, which is *Rampant*!

§ ii. *WILLIAM GAMAGE'S IDLE BRAINS*
William gamege his idle Braines

My Louing frendes that love to playe,
vse not the hooling game by daye
ffrom the night[1] I take yt best.
when all the birdes are in theyr neaste
yet I doe live in quiett rest
and thinke my hooling game the best

And louing ffrends I cannot chose
but now leaue off all sports to vse.
only[2] paper yncke and penn
to write the sportes of wells may men.
yet I doe Live &c.

which now in shorte I will recyte
As fast as I with penn can write
And bring the same vnto my mynde
you shall therein[3] these may games ffynde
yet I doe Live &c.

Nowe first the Lord of May cam in,
with all his men attending him,
with true loves knottes, most finely knitte
and euery thing most ffyne and neate[4]
Yet doe I &c.

You virgins all whoe of euery sorte[5]
whoe with yor welth[6] mayntayne the sporte
greve not thoughe some at yt[7] doe frowne
they live not loved in our Towne,
yet doe I &c.

the musicke in yor dawnsing[8] sporte
was ioye vnto the greater sorte
that was to all such great delight[9]
that none wold parte out of theyr sight[10]
yet doe I &c.

[1] *but in the night.*   [2] *saue only.*   [3] *heerin.*
[4] *most braue and fitte.*   [5] *all of everye sorte.*
[6] *in yor wells...our.*   [7] *therat.*   [8] *and their dauncing.*
[9] *greue not though some ther be yt spurne.*
[10] *ytt doth to ther disgraces turne.*

The worldlike captaynes[1] stowte and bowlde
cam there theyr meetings to beholde[2],
marching along with all theyr trayne[3]
throughout the towne and backe agayne,
yet doe I &c.

The gallant pinner with good regarde
cam with his men as yt was harde
singing a song of Wakefilde greene.
and had great prayse where he was seene,
yet doe I &c.

And Robyn whoode was likewise seene
with all his gallants arrayed in greene.[4]
theyr arrowes were a long cloth yarde[5]
yf yt be true as I hav harde
yet doe I &c.

A Sparked Calfe as I hard saye
was brought vnto them in theyr Maye.[6]
but afterwards was slayne in fight
for darkning of the way to light
yet doe I &c.

drumes fyfes and trompetts did sowne apace
the contrye held at no disgrace[7]
vnto our towne to make resorte
to heare the Roaring cannot[8] shotte
yet doe I &c.

Our gallant mynded marshall trayne
did in the crosse[9] our sporte maynteyne
and yeke St George did greatly grace,
with thundering peaces in that place,
yet doe I &c.

---

[1] *warlike Captaines.*   [2] *ther merye meetting did vphold.*
[3] *& marche Alonge with all his trayne.*
[4] *brave & green.*   [5] *a Just clothe yeard.*
[6] *was brought to shewe vnto theire Maye; was brought for show*
   annother daye.
[7] *held that no disgrace.*   [8] *canon; channon.*   [9] *one the crose*

Then did St George of Wells proceade
with all his knights most brave in deed
theyr Irishe foatemen did attende,
and all men did the same comende
yet doe I &c.

Then cam also two men in heare
betwixe them boathe one egge[1] did beare,
and each of them a forked post
for to preserve that egge from loste,
yet doe I &c.

and were not these well laden men
that bare an egge[2] betwixt them then
vpon a Coldstaffe[3] and two restes
to ease theyr sholders when they list
yet doe I &c.

Olde Grandam bunche, that filthe and slutte[4]
had in one pott a fylthye gutt.
and puddings made as she went, through[5]
all the Towne in a wheele barrowe,
yet doe I &c.

Acteon from man converted was
into a harte and soe did passe
along the streetes and seene of all
and all him chaste to see him ffall[6]
yet doe I live &c.

Diana sometymes[7] fayer and bright
with sixe Nimphes cloathed all in white
rode in a Coach in stately sorte,
as all men can the same reporte
yet doe I &c.

Likewise in white there were sixe men
which carried Voath[8] statly then
at Worke and framing of an arcke
which pleased all them that hyt did marke[9]
yet doe I Live &c.

---

[1] one eye; yt eye. [2] one eye. [3] a Coulstaffe.
[4] filthy slutt; yt clenly slutt. [5] thurrow. [6] his fall.
[7] Diana sumptuous. [8] Noach; Noah. [9] which did it marke.

The gyante and Gyantes[1]
in loftly maner loked presice[2]
on after the other by degree
which was most pleasant for to see
yet doe I &c.

[3]Be fore these gianntts ther·did goe
by art a naked fethered boye
who in his hand a sword did beare
still making roome before them ther
yet I &c.

ffower gallant knightes two of a syde
before the Egipt king did ryde
eight yrishe footemen pages were
attending on the kinge most rare.
yet doe I &c.

The Egipt king in ritch array
roade on a gallant steade that day
and Carried was his Queene so rytche
as neuer there was[4] any such
yet doe I &c.

also there might many a man
have seene the place[5] most stately then
brought in, A page out[6] throughe the Towne
by eight in Lawne with great renowne,
yet doe I &c.

then instantly vpon the same
came many there[7] of worthie fame
to shewe theyr louingnes in sight
as yt appeared then that night
yet doe I &c.

Then presently insued the meat
theree hondred dishes through the street,
vnto the place where there was spent
mony Lardgly to good intent
yet doe I &c.

---

[1] *giauntt & the giauntise* (=giantess).
[2] *In lustie manner tooke presese; lofty.*
[3] Supplied from the second copy of the Bill. But see below, p. 183.
[4] *here was.*   [5] *the plate; ye plate.*   [6] *in a pageant.*   [7] *many a man.*

This beinge done which there is sayed[1]
all then repayer homewards made
the fyery dragon laye in wayte
for to devowre the princes[2] streight,
yet doe I &c.

but I St George of wells comende
and all his knights that did attende
that wrought the dragons great decaye
and saved the princes lief that day
yet doe I &c.

Our Cittizens gallant grave and wise
cam to our sporte and sawe our prize.[3]
they did also the same frequent
enioyed thereby in mynds content
yet doe I &c.

An other day a shewe was made
with tinckers and with men of trade
A hatter and a grocer then there
were seene on horseback sylling ware,
yet doe I &c.

Also a spynner that did ryde
two vsurers likewise all in pryde,
that they theyr mony wold have lende
but all in vayne and to no ende
yet doe I &c.

ffor they did lend yt at such rate
as wold vndoe a man of state,
No man wold deale at any hande
for feare of forfeiting theyr bonde
yet doe I &c.

All things here in each degree
did please both Towne and Countrye
without offence at all to any
but was comended much of many
yet doe I &c.

[1] *here is said.*   [2] *the princesse.*   [3] *the prize.*

Nowe podding wives haue lost theyr trade,
and hatters they begynne[1] to fade
the spynners Twornes[2] are held in scorne
and vsurers are hardley borne
yet doe I &c.

but I as dutie byndes comende
and him I loved as my frende
whoe me at hooles so well preferred
that nowe therefore I lye in Warde
yet doe I &c.

Before these paggens[3] there did goe
by arte a naked fethered boye
whoe in his hande a sworde did beare
still making rome before them there
yet doe I &c.

Nowe for the gentile I will praye
which kept vs company all the may
and never lefte vs to thende
that good may[4] euer those defende;
yet god graunt that all may live in rest
with ioye to saye my game is best

finis.

December 6. 1608[5]

Memorandum that this writinge was shewed vnto Wm. Gamadge vppon his examinacon in his Maiestyes Courte of Starr Chamber.

W. Portburye.

§ iii. *THE QUINTESSENCE OF WIT*

The Quintessence of Witt or P.P.P.

Tell me of flesh, Tutt, no, giue me the fysh,
the heatinge oyster, and the spawne of godds,[6]
The Crudytty of Lobsters, is the dysh
that soe exceeds all other fry by odds.
thus Mounseir Lechers secreat fyshy sleight:

---

[1] *hatters doe begynne.*   [2] *tournes.*   [3] *Pageants.*
[4] *that god may.*   [5] from copy A.   [6] *codds.*

is but to styrre his fleshly appytitte
Softe who goes ther, whatt p, P, and P,
poxe, puncke, and purittan? the dyvell yt is,
and may be soe; for Sir some tymes we see,
poxe, plageth Puncke, for Purittans amyse.
well, be yt as twill Ile not presyzely tell
but yet me thinks yt iumpeth wondros well.
What holloe hoo, ye pampred Asyian Iades,
must men of not and worth be yor Comrades?
How groes yt, those more base[1] then stynge, and fflyrt?
are thus become soe prowd and malapert?
Shall every Rascole, and vile Jobbernole,
A Cytties quintessence of wytt Controle?
stayeninge the greatnes of his reputacon
in scurvile Jestes in such a busie fashion
boldly reproueinge to the verye face
his secret vices to his huge disgrace
yf yt be so naye it[2] must be so
aucthoritie shall in his fulnes shewe
his furious vigour of incensed wrath
vnsheates[3] yt selfe, mercye no entrance hath
but what sterne Justice giues, & wooden stockes
can minister for such rebellious folkes
neither Regard of Conscience nor of pittie
Nor the stricte bond of a pure societie
shall by heavens Azure welkinge once aswage
yee smallest sparckle of my furious rage[4]
tis not your horned horse the hungry soules
nor the weake gambols[5] of yor pigeon holes
shall buckler you or anie[6] that manure it
Can fleshe composed of muddie earth indure it,
Rather then I will beare so vile yle[7] suffringe thrall
Ile spend my flatt capp pouch & horse & all
whie what care I to compasse my intente
Much wealthe be loste much tyme vp ont be spente
in Informacon trottinge to & fro
to skuld to veaze[8] to hackney come & goe

[1] *yt men more base.*   [2] *naye yf it.*   [3] *vnshethes.*
[4] *my burninge rage.*   [5] *gamble.*   [6] *nor anie.*
[7] *yle=ill?*   [8] *to scudd, to veze.*

I value yt not fower galliard friskyn skipps
to spend therein & hundred golden shipps[1]
to reobtaine by it my Creditts wynninge
I hold yt not so much as veniall synninge
thus talkinge Campant[2] one of madd condicon
standes nymblie vp made rouffe[3] of lowe submission
& said thy pride & stubborn insolence
doth meritt nought but scorninge & expence
Ist possible that Captaine Fa, va, va[4]
Camelion like is turned apostata
by sweete St John he is like a ffelters hatt
turned wrongeside outward But[5] woot you what
he dares not looke a pigney[6] in the face
much lesse a giantt or a dragons a..e
nay more then that[7] he cannot broke the noyse
of flute or fife or Trumpetts statelie voyce
nor can he once abide the stroake of drumbe
nor smoake of powder but the smoake[8] of some
A gun quoth he[9] hands of forbeare forbeare
his reasons good twill burne his ladie warne[10]
hes growne so ympotent he cannot weld
his launce nor pike nor scarce can beare his shield
Butt yet potenciall he can breake his speare
in venus darlinge with a full Carreare

---

[1] *golden chapps; & = an.*
[2] *Rampant.*
[3] *made Condjie of (Condjie = congee).*
[4] *Captaine ta-ra-ra.*
[5] *But Sir.* [6] *pygmaye.*
[7] *more yf that.*
[8] *= the smocke.* [9] *a gon quod you.*
[10] *ware.*

Chapter V

THE LIBEL PROPER

(i) *The Libel*

It is evident that there was a close connection between specifically dramatic forms of entertainment, with satiric intent at least in part, and satire in other forms. The play of *Keep the Widow Waking* went along with two ballads celebrating the same events, one of them, a satirical ballad, being actually the reflection of the play and composed by a spectator of the play. The writer of *Michael and Frances* was probably a well-known local hand at satirical ballad-writing. At Wells the dramatic pageant was set forth in narrative form to preserve its memory, and in the meantime to recall the revels in retrospect to those who had been present or to introduce others to some faint image of their splendour and mirth. And the element of civic and religious strife that entered into those revels also inspired the writing of a formal satire which was closely linked up with the May Game and the ballad, and which in its manner and its quality brings us near to literature of the time which justly has claimed the attention of critics and historians. We may remember how, in the higher reaches of the London literary world, Lodge, Ben Jonson and Marston dipped their pens in critical gall both for formal satire and for satiric drama.

We may well, therefore, be led to consider drama and verse-satire as complementary parts of a considerable mass of literature that gained its savour from personal attacks, more or less disguised. And it may well be that the growing wave of formal satire in the hands of emulators of Juvenal and

Martial spread through the provinces to give a new turn to the ambitions of local poetasters, hitherto content with ballad and jig.

It is interesting to observe that the Star Chamber began to be appealed to more and more frequently during the last decade of the sixteenth century for redress against libellous attacks. This kind of business in the Court, indeed, reached its maximum during the last years of Queen Elizabeth. This was precisely, we may notice, the period of the rise and growth of literary satire in the world of printed books, in the hands of Lodge, Hall, Donne and Marston. It is also the period of prose satire, as it appears in the history of literature, of the Marprelate Tracts, or of the Nashe-Harvey controversy. Printed literature, in fact, offers a parallel to the course of what we might call underground literature in the form of libels.

When we consider the draconian severity of Archbishop Whitgift's edict of 1599, ordering certain satires in print to be burned and forbidding the printing of 'satires or epigrams' henceforth, we should clearly do well to take into account the flood of elaborate literary satire that was filling the Court of Star Chamber. Such satire was frequently engaged in stimulating religious enmities and local feuds, giving rise to breaches of the peace, and bringing more difficulties to the already sufficiently onerous task of governing the country.

Falstaff explains a procedure that was only too frequently pursued by any Elizabethan anxious to injure an enemy; he is addressing Prince Hal:

An I have not ballads made on you all and sung to filthy tunes, let a cup of sack be my poison.

Sir John Harington, again, in his *Diary* notes privately his vengeful intentions after the same fashion:

I will write a damnable storie and put it in goodlie verse about Lord A. He hath done me some ill turnes.

To which note he appends the unconscionable comment:

God keepe us from lyinge and slander worke.

London and the printed satire set models that were only too acceptable to provincial disaffection seeking an outlet or nursing a grudge. It put a new weapon into the hands of those who sought to destroy enemies by the cruel laughter of ridicule and caricature published abroad in various ways, ministering to subversive delight among partisan sympathisers. One of the stock accusations against the willing hearer of a libel is that he has read or listened to it and did 'rejoice thereat', the measure of his joy being the measure of his guilt.

The two examples of such libels which I have chosen will show clearly enough how far satire could reflect party animosities and be used as a means of attack, as a move in a game which might well take an ugly and dangerous turn.

The first has the especial interest that attaches to any connection with Shakespeare or with the society in which he moved at Stratford. The angry feud with which this libel is concerned was of long standing, though the libel itself dates from 1619, three years after Shakespeare's death.

(ii) *The Old Guard at Stratford*

§ i. RIOTS AT STRATFORD

It is well known that Shakespeare's father was fined for recusancy. The debate will probably never be settled whether John Shakespeare was a Catholic or a Puritan recusant. Nor does his son declare to us through his plays or his poetry that he himself stood in the ranks of either faction of extremists. Yet the question was one that rent Stratford and Warwickshire in twain in Shakespeare's lifetime. It is most reasonable to believe that Shakespeare kept to the middle course of conformity with the established church, by virtue of political

convictions if not of religious. For the Church of England
then as now harboured a wide variety of shades of religious
faith, brought in Elizabeth's day into the one fold by the
paramount need for national unity. It would be equally
unreasonable, however, to question the poet's attachment
to old customs, his mistrust of innovation, and above all his
dislike of the new discipline that was seeking to remodel the
life of England to the pattern of Geneva. He could not but
be aware of the trend of things in Stratford during the last
years of his life, for his own friends and connections were
deeply involved in the controversy, which came to a head
shortly after his death in 1616.

On 16 March 1619 Thomas Wilson was made Vicar of
Stratford, in place of John Rogers, who was superseded on
the ground of plurality or at least on that pretext. On 22
May Wilson was instituted by the Bishop of Worcester into
the Vicarage. It was agreed between Wilson and Rogers
that Wilson should be inducted on Monday, 31 May, and
that on the Sunday Rogers should take his last evening service,
at which Wilson should attend but take no part. In the meantime Stratford was agog with excitement at the supersession
of a popular and easy-going Vicar, a member of an old and
numerous Stratford family, by one who was known to be a
rigid precisian, and was a foreign importation. Angry
passions were awakened, and plots were laid. The Sunday
evening came. The congregation was in the church, including Alderman Henry Smith, the church officials, and the
Constables. In the midst of evening prayer the noise of a
riot was heard and a clamour outside of confused objurgations and threats to the new Vicar, whom the rioters accused
of evil living and incontinency. 'Hange him, kill him, pull
out his throate,...lett vs pull dragg and hale him out of the
Church', they cried. The mob was armed with swords,
daggers, forest bills, pikes and stones. Henry Smith, who
was a Justice of the Peace, went to the church door and
charged them to go home peaceably, having taken the pre-

caution to lock up Wilson in the chancel to ensure his safety. The rioters paid no attention to Smith, and when he had the church doors shut, tried to force them, and threw big stones through the windows. But in the end no great harm was done to life or limb.

The list of rioters accused in the Attorney-General's Star Chamber Bill may well be examined with interest. It includes almost every name that we know to have been closely associated with Shakespeare, among others Hathaway, Nash, Lane, Reynolds and Court.[1] The first two named, indeed, are John Nash and William Reynolds, to each of whom, at his death, Shakespeare had left money to buy memorial rings, as to his London actor friends and fellows. One may well guess where his sympathies lay in the general controversy, however deeply he would have deplored such recourse to violence. For in his attitude towards riot, as shown in his plays, we make one of our few certain contacts with Shakespeare's own convictions.

There were other counts in the accusation of violent opposition to lawful authority among the men of Stratford. For time out of mind a horse fair had been held in Stratford on the green on the way to the church. The fair was duly held in the May following the riot, as usual. And on 1 May, as usual, a Summer Pole or Maypole was set up in the fair ground. The city officials found the way blocked by the Maypole, forcing carts and beasts on to 'a fair pavement' meant for the use of citizens going to church or coming from it. Wherefore, when the next fair was held, in September, John Wilmore, Bailiff of Stratford, and Alderman Henry Smith had the pole taken down, alleging that it was a public nuisance and in any case could be set up elsewhere.

---

[1] The full list is 'John Nashe. William Reynolds, Thomas Rutter, Richard Wyatt, John Lane, gents, John Rogers, John Pincke, William Nixon, William Hathaway, yeomen, Thomas Wills, Weaver; Thomas Court, Blacksmith; William Smith, Maltster; Raphe Smith Haberdasher, Joane Askewe, wife of Richard Askewe'.

A second riot ensued. Some forty supporters of Maypoles gathered together, and with great outcry set the pole up again in triumph, to the great detriment of law and order.

The inconvenience of Maypoles was, of course, the least important aspect of this conflict to the Puritan governors of Stratford. Maypoles, together with all similar manifestations of ancient and joyful custom in English life, were anathema to their rigid moral discipline. The Maypole was brought into town or village with ceremony and with song, it was bedecked with garlands and ribbons, and men and maidens danced round it. It was a centre of merriment. But to the Puritans, to Stubbes or Northbrooke as to Wilmore, Smith and Wilson, it was a relic both of heathendom and of Popery, as well as of moral evil. The pole itself was an idol, set up for worship by men of sin. So Northbrooke wrote in language that would meet with the approval of Mrs Yard in Wells, as of the Stratford precisians:

What adoe make our yong men at the time of May? Do they not use night-watchings to rob and steal young trees out of other men's grounds and bring them into their parishe, with minstrels playing before: and when they have set it up, they will deck it with floures and garlands, and dance rounde (men and women togither, moste unseemely and intolerable, as I have proved before) about the tree, like unto the children of Israel that daunced about the golden calfe that they had set up. (*Treatise against Dicing and Dancing*, 1577, p. 140.)

To such a pitch did local tyranny prevail that Charles I found it necessary to enact and declare the lawfulness of Maypoles, in 1633. In 1644 the Long Parliament swooped down upon these monuments of 'heathenish vanity' and ordered their destruction.

It fell to Charles II to authorize the return of this cherished fragment of ancient mirth. But indeed his return was anticipated when on 1 May 1660, as Pepys tells us, 'they were very merry at Deale, setting up the King's flags upon one of their Maypoles'.

These two outbreaks of mob-law in Stratford were, in fact, closely related to one another, both being demonstrations against the strangling grip of the Puritan governing faction in the town. It was inevitable that the feeling should seek expression in other ways. And a series of libels gave utterance, in defamatory satire, to the seething indignation of the contrary faction.

Three of these fragments of underground literature are reproduced here with one small necessary omission in the second. No attempt is made in the Bill to indicate the possible authors of those quoted here, who must have been Stratford men. Not only are they familiar with the matters in question, but intimately acquainted with the butts of their satire, as we may see for example in the vivid little caricature of Richard Castle, the 'monster with four elbows'. The literary intention is evident, especially in the 'Sonnet' which laments the unhappy case of Rogers and which reflects the advice of Polonius to 'trye and then trust', as the first 'Satyre' reflects the image of the 'galled jade' in *Hamlet*. The trend of thought is by no means crystal clear in either instance. But the general position is unmistakable, and is expressed with a certain force and verve. There is no question that they stung their enemies painfully. Another libel of a grosser kind, written by one John Pinke, and not here printed, suggested that the father of the lawyer Thomas Lucas had 'learned to carry coals', as if, the Bill remarks indignantly, Lucas was a collier's son, whereas he was in fact a gentleman, well descended by birth and parentage. And in general, the Bill is obliging enough to annotate the libels and to identify their objects after the fashion of many a scene in a stage-play of comic effect. The new Vicar recognized himself instantly when Pinke wrote mentioning a rogue: 'by the word (Rouge) is meant...Thomas Wilson Clerke', we are told. And Henry Smith and John Wolmer, Aldermen both, are as anxious as Dogberry that it should be remembered that they are 'just-asses', and they have even seen to it that it should be written down!

§ ii. *A SATIRE TO THE CHIEF RULERS*

A Satyre to the Cheife rulers in the
Synagogue of Stratford

Stratford is a Towne that doeth make a great shewe,
but yet it is governed but by a fewe.
O Jesus Christe of heaven,
I thincke they are but Seaven,
Puritants without doubt,
for you may knowe them they are soe stout.
They saye tis noe sinne their neighbours howse to take,
but such lawes their father the devill did make,
These men seeme of a puer faction
but like the devill in dissemblacion,
as smooth as oyle outward, In words,
but within they are full of dissencion and discords,
but woe be to those whited walles,
they are the cause of all these brales,
A heavy curse (o lord) vpon them
and because they haue bereft vs of our best freinde,
and in his steede here haue they plast,
A fellow[1] that hath neither shame nor grace,
yet these men are true religious without Quirkes,
ffor one of the Cheifest hath red far in Perkins workes,
The rest are deepe dissemblinge hypocrites,
that in good workes haue noe delites,
but their delighte is to doe wronge
but yet they bere a flatteringe toungue.
but soft my sater[2] be not too free,
for thou will make them spourne at thee,
for rubb a horse where scabbes be thicke,
and thou wilt make him winse and kicke,
but softe bethincke thee wheres the cause,
they saye they doe nothinge but lawes,
but suer the lawes they doe wrest,
for to bringe poore people in distresse,
bee suer their lawier[3] is of god accurst,

---

[1] 'Meaning Thomas Wilson', according to the Bill.
[2] I.e. satire.   [3] 'Meaning Thomas Lucas.'

for hee begune this mischeife first,
and with his malice and his spite
was first that brought this Lapse to light,
but a dubble woe be vpon him
that did this matter first beginne,
these men applye themselues to the lawe,
because theyd keepe the poor in awe,
O lord doe then revenge the poor,
and their right again to them restore,
have these hypocrites mischeife bread
if that their minister[1] be knockt ath head
for if that hee continue longe,
and will not make amends for this wronge
he shall never gett the peoples love
while he lives on earth in god as aboue
and so my verses here shall rest,
I praye god turne all to the best.

§ iii. *REVENGE STILL BROTHER ROGERS*
SHALL NOT LIVE

Revenge still brother Rogers shall not live,
maye I not live, o whoe will with mee mourne,
assist my woe, whilst woe on mee doth last,
whoe will releiue my woe, my hearte doth burne,
To see mans state wanes as the winde doth turne,
He warrs, and winns, and wynninge lost by strife.
warr is an other death, a sure vncertayne life,
trye and then trust, giue creditt by delaye:
the feyned freinds, with feyned lookes betraye,
Baker[2] had never lived to vanquish mee,
Had it not bene for Lucas trecherye.
Shall I of Chaundler,[3] and busye William[4] speake?
that badd to make a tale, and that to breake,
hence I conclude what all the world doth see,

[1] 'Meaning Mr Wilson' again.
[2] Daniel Baker, Alderman.
[3] William Chandler, Alderman. The two Aldermen, said the malcontents, 'had noe more conscience then doggs'.
[4] 'by (busye Willm) is meant...William Smith Haberdasher.'

there is noe peace where is noe vnitye,
Though I on earth for thee receiue disgrace,
liue I in heaven see Jesus face to face.
The burden of this Sonnet
    June, July August, and September,
      although he come he shall not mortefie one member.

§ iv. *TO ANY HONEST PURITAN*

To any honest Puritant where you finde him

Sirrah ho, the greattest newes since the . . .
that all the old bitinge and young sucking Puritans of Stratford,
are ioyned with their twoo Just-asis a peace, maliciously to dis-
place and vtter vndoe their minister, and to bringe in his place as
arrand a k:[1] as them selues of purpose to assist them in their
hypocrisye, And now seinge they haue sett all the towne together
by the eares, which is the true office of a Puritant, and fyndinge
their plott hath not their wisht effecte, it is thought that diverse
of them will runne horne madd, therefore I would haue thee to
make haste vp hither to begg them,[2] But if thou be not private
thy purpose wilbe smelt out by some longe-nosd knave or other,
but be not thou violent like them, but learne to reade in Perkin
workes they will teach thee patience; and doe not skibb at any
of them, for then they would saye that were more then needes,
therefore it is very ill to be accompted too busie,[3] or to shewe
like a monster with fower elbowes,[4] or for a Cobler to turn
devine,[5] or any great officer to turne dissembler,[6] but some death
vnconscionable knaues will harken to nothinge but to fulfill

---

[1] Thomas Wilson: 'thereby terminge him an arrant knave'.
[2] I.e. to make suit for guardianship and disposal of their goods, as
lunatics.
[3] William Smith, haberdasher: 'whom they conceived to be a busye
person'.
[4] Richard Castle, weaver: 'because he vseth in his gate or goeinge as
some obserue, to shake his elbowes'.
[5] John Jordan, shoemaker, of Stratford.
[6] John Wolmer and Henry Smith, both J. P.s: 'whoe are also intended
by the said ridiculous words in dirision of them and there places (twoo
Justasses a peace) in the said libell mentioned'.

their greedy desires. Therefore farewell from Romalye this merry moneth of Maye: Thy honest freind, if thou doe not turne Puritant. ff: S:.[1]

(iii) *Hudibras in Nottingham*

§ i. CIVIC DUDGEON

On 24 March 1617, the fourteenth anniversary of the accession of King James, a reminder came to his officers that the ancient religious dissensions of his country were still active and troublesome. If danger to his life had come from Catholic discontents in earlier years, the growing obstinacy of the Puritan sects gave strength to disruptive influences which in the end brought down the monarchy itself under his son Charles I. But nonconformity was still a minor peril. And the King's Attorney-General was ready to take up the cause of certain Nottingham citizens complaining of libel at the hands of a rival faction, even though the substance of the libels was an accusation of schismatic Puritanism.

The libelled citizens were men of apparent worth and standing. Anker Jackson was 'an ancient Alderman', several times Mayor of the City of Nottingham. George Jackson was his son. Richard Caldwell was a clergyman, 'a zealous preacher of the word of god' in the same town, 'licenciated and appointed by the Lords grace of Yorke'. George Cotes was the parson of St Peter's Church there. William Hopkyn was a draper. And Mrs Margaret Willson was a respectable married woman. It was intolerable that such persons should be pilloried as they were, the two Jacksons as Caiaphas and St George respectively, Caldwell as Jonas, either Cotes or Hopkyn as Dildo (the attribution is in question), and Mrs Willson as St Megg, with such implications as appear plainly enough in the libels, quite apart from the general damaging assertion that they all 'leave the Church to Conventicle'.

On the other hand, the libellers were of equal standing

---

[1] I cannot identify the author from these initials.

for the most part. Thomas Nixe or Nickes was also an Alderman, and had lately been Mayor. He was indeed, it appears,
actually in office at the time of the first publication of the
libels. William Hansby and Francis Withington were also
Nottingham clergymen, and Withington's brother William,
who evidently was the author of one at least of the two libels,
is described as 'gentleman', as are also Gervase Mason and
Gervase Eyre, members of ancient families of the county.
Christopher Strelley also bore a famous name, though he was
a goldsmith. We descend lower in the social scale with
Thomas Aldred the apothecary and William Martindale the
spurrier. And Robert Leake was only a vintner, servant to
Mr Collishaw who kept a tavern. But Mayor is confronting
Mayor, and pulpit meets pulpit in this debate. It is evidently
a war of factions in Nottingham's civic world, of such
factions as riddled every city in England, all divided by religious dissensions, in which for the most part a Puritan party
was fought, not by the Anglican Church party, but by those
of Catholic sympathies. So it was here.

If Jackson and his faction are accused of 'conventicling',
they retort with accusations of Catholicism to discredit their
opponents. And not without reason. William Withington,
when interrogated whether he attends the Church by law
established, and how often during the last seven years he has
heard a sermon or taken the Sacrament, evades the question on
the plea of irrelevancy. But the Court had already made up
its mind. To each of the defendants examined is put an unusual
interrogatory as an appendix, which the Court allowed.

'Have you', they are asked, 'in your deposition, equivocated
or reserved or saved to yor self by mentall reservacion, or by
collusion otherwaies, any phrase, speeche sentence matter or
thinge to avoide weaken or hinder the truth.'

An absurd device, truly. For an equivocator could as well
equivocate on this question as on any other.

The suit ran a deliberate course in the Court, depositions

being taken at intervals from December 1618 to November 1620. And sentence was given on 30 June 1621. This fact is recorded on an endorsement, but there is no record of the sentence. We do not even know which way the verdict went. But the Attorney-General himself was the prosecutor on behalf of the Jackson clan. And the evidence of the last witnesses called told heavily against the accused.

There was, in fact, no real doubt that the weapon of libel had been used in the quarrel of these Nottingham factions, and no real doubt that the generally admitted expositions of the libellous texts were correct. It is certain, by his own reported confession, that William Withington was the poet of the second libel, and probably of the first too. And the libels had unquestionably furnished his faction, and Nottingham at large, considerable mirth and enjoyment.

Martindale the spurrier and others formed themselves into a party of waits, with an improvised orchestra of candlesticks, tongs and basins, and bawled one of the songs forth in the night through the streets of the town. They were well received here and there, for example at Fabian Drew's house, and in front of Mr Gombleby's house, and had been invited to enter and give a private performance by Mr Wightman, whose two daughters with their father formed an appreciative audience. There were also more sophisticated renderings. The song had been set to music, 'prickt in 4 parts to the vyalls', says the Rev. Mr Hansby, who heard it sung at Mr Greaves' house. And there seems to have been a notable evening's revelry in the cellar of Collishaw's tavern, when Eyre, the Masons, the Withingtons and others, with Leake busy supplying drink to them, 'did there laughe and were merry' with the song, led in their singing by one Hacket or Hacklet, apparently a professional entertainer. Several of the accused confess to having sung 'part of the song'. And there can be no question but that this means that each bore his part in a four man song. For a parallel to this scene, at ten o'clock of the night, we may well go to *Twelfth Night*, when Sir Toby, Sir Andrew and Feste made the welkin dance indeed and squeaked out their coziers' catches without any mitigation or remorse of voice.

For both these exploits some of the executants were complained of and brought before the Mayor. The Mayor was Thomas Nixe, who was careful to bind them over to be of good behaviour. One might marvel therefore to find Alderman Nixe among the defendants. But the last witness of all, William Clarke, mercer, of Nottingham, tells how the Mayor was in an alehouse at a Fair held at Lenton, and there called for a piper and bade him sing the libellous song. The piper refused, and began to sing another less dangerous song, hoping for the best. But Nixe silenced him, saying 'that's not the song, I meant the song of the Puritans of Nottingham', bade him go fetch another, more willing piper, and in the meantime took his pipes from him as a hostage. And it appears that Nixe laughed heartily and rejoiced, when the right piper came and sang the song required, though it were in disgrace of the Alderman's brethren. Seated in his Justice's chair, a wink and a nod must have heartened the rioters when he bound them over. But it was all very subversive of law and order in Nottingham.

I am afraid that Alderman Nixe's mirth was not due only to what Aldred the apothecary suggested as the adequate excuse for his own laughter, 'in regard of the straungeness and conceyted tune sett to it'. The tune actually was that known as *Bonny Nell*, it appears. Nixe is further accused of having dealt in some odd kind of black magic against Jackson. He is said to have taken a stick or rod and to have drawn in the ashes of the fire in his own house a picture or image of his enemy, in the presence of others. It is clearly the same kind of sympathetic magic that we find in the making of wax images of the person whom it is desired to destroy by wasting. Doubtless the accusation, whether true or false, was intended to appeal to King James' notorious fear and hatred of witchcraft.

William Withington, the poet of the party, is evidently a hot anti-Puritan, and in his evidence enlarges upon the theme of his songs. His enemies have all formerly been cited before the Archbishop of York for nonconformity, and have been fined by him. They have held private meetings in Alderman Jackson's house at night

and have there expounded places of scripture according to their owne fancies and prayed of their owne heads together without the forme of prayer prescribed and catachised each other in the matter of Religion after their own fashion and out of their owne heads and fancies.

They are known in Nottingham as *Proecisians*, much given to such clandestine assemblies as Withington hates, and they have

vppon Sondayes and other tymes as well by night as by daye wilfully left and forsaken the Service and sermons of their owne parochiall Minister and Preacher in their proper parishes and traveled 5. or 6 myles distant to heare the Sermons and exercises of other sectaries which were of their humorous faction.

What else Withington wished to convey is best studied in the literary versions of his views.

Here we cannot fail to observe how close a parallel there is between the controversies alive in these debates and those of a later generation. The Nottingham of 1617 is not far from the Nottingham where Charles I raised his standard against the Roundheads, whom Butler was to lash in his mercilessly witty satire. Nor is it a mere coincidence that the metre of the first of these libels is precisely the metre of *Hudibras*. There is much of the spirit, and something of the wit, of *Hudibras* in it also. This poet too can turn a grotesque rhyme to comic effect. And some of the distiches might, if put to a competent critic, be unhesitatingly ascribed to Butler, with no discredit to the later satirist:

> Ile do him right were he a Scott,
> hele Chant a Psalme and drinke a Pott.
> But when he should the text expound,
> the Hogsheads full it cannot sound.

But the Nottingham man is the more kindly. He still can hope for the conversion of his enemies to true love of their King and commonwealth.

§ ii. *MY MUSE ARISE AND TRUTH THEN TELL*

Better to be song, then to be redd to the tune of Bonny Nell:

My muse arise and truth then tell;
of a Pure secte that sprang from hell,
who are so vaine soe false and fickle
they leave the Church to Conventicle;
on huge[1] Sct Anker they lay hould
who is an hipocrite most bould:
He travells often to Jordaine,
where, in the lord he taketh gaine.
Ile do him right were he a Scott,
hele Chant a Psalme and drinke a Pott.
But when he should the text expound,
the Hogsheads full it cannot sound:
I pitty much that vpsett Joanas
who is so ledd as never non was
by hipocrites and bawdy Queanes,
who would be sainted by his meanes,
but I will giue the man his dew,
he is to honest for their crew:
the next in order doth ensew,
the sacredst person in this stew
Sct Margaret that doth excell:
Sct Winifride for all her well:
She hath a founte where manie thinke;
the great Sct Gorge his fill doth drinke:
Neare to this fountaine I haue hard,
one sells Divinity by the yard,
for be she baude or be she hore,
she takes vpp all vppon the score;
if she be faire and pure in speech,
she paies her brother on her breech
Theis sectaries love noe confession
nor can indure the ould profession,

[1] *Hugh.*

by night they Catichise each other
the holy sister with the brother,
and when the high preest hath well druncke
each one betakes him to his puncke
Some Handicrafters by there trade,
have Gospellers by them ben made
the Coblers and the Tailors proude,
for Conventicklers are allowed,
theis Mechanickes are very nimble,
to leape beyond there laste and thimble:
But cease my muse here take thy rest
of their Conversion hope the best,
in love to those that haue trew zeale,
that love the king and Comon weale,
I wishe all those that do not soe,
to this dammed Conventicle goe:

§ iii. *MARY'S CHURCH*

Maries Church

Brethren goe home and praie,
for wee haue lost a daie
the wicked beare the swaie,
Maries Church wee haue loste
with noe smale charge no cost.

Caiphas doth make greate moane,
the profett wilbe gone
and he be left all alone
Maries Church &c.

Jonas is refused
and lookes like one is dead
Noe learning is in his head
Maries Church &c.

Sisters yor greif is mickle
for time hath with his sickle
Cutt off yor Conventicle
Maries Church &c.

See that you morne in blacke,
for the poore temples racke,
and doe Crie out a lacke,
Maries Church &c.

Sct George hath broke his lavnce
his Cutt doth leape and praunce
Sct Megg lies in a traunce
Maries Church &c.

Dildo leave to expound
full flatt vppon the ground,
and sing out like a hound
Maries Church &c.

All you that be precise,
and dailie Catekise,
Send out yor dolefull cries,
Maries Church &c.

How this befell alas
wee must recorde in brasse
and praie for Church Nicholas
Maries Church &c.

Thus for to end in myter[1]
Lett vs praie for Church Peter
that the wicked never meeter[2]
Maries Church wee have lost
with the[3] smale Charge noe cost

[1] *meeter* (=metre).   [2] *meete her*, i.e. the Church (?).   [3] *noe*.

APPENDIX

I. *SUMMARY OF ORIGINAL SOURCES*

(An asterisk denotes a primary document in each case)

Chap. II.   (i) *The Old Joiner of Aldgate*

PUBLIC RECORD OFFICE:

Star Chamber; *Proceedings,* * 8. 8/2; 5. P. 5/6; 5. P. 65/10;
5. M. 15/40; 8. 249/17.
Court of Requests; *Requests,* I. 28, 29, 110; II. 402/79.
Chancery; C. 24. 182, I/*Sharles* v. *Seymour*; 290/30; 312/43;
C. 2. J.I. H. 9/41; C. 33. 96, 107, 109; C. 142. 265/56;
236/58.
Court of Delegates; *Delegates,* 5/3, 13, 41, 67.
State Papers; *S.P.* 38, vols. 2, 7, 8, 44, 48.
Privy Council; *A.P.C.* 1582–98.

SOMERSET HOUSE:

P.C.C. Drury 61; *Wallopp* 75, 79; *Dorset* 84.

(ii) *Keep the Widow Waking*

PUBLIC RECORD OFFICE:

Star Chamber; *Proceedings,* * 8. 31/16; 8. 296/20; 5. H. 31/34.
Chancery; C. 24. 45/*Munds* v. *Colford*; 228/47; 262/50; 292/43;
443/34; 497/*Bingham* v. *Bonham*; C. 2. J.I. C. 1/33;
Proceedings, 1621–25, II. 339/62.
Composition Books, 1554–94, fols. 131 b, 133.

SOMERSET HOUSE:

P.C.C. Scrope 97.
Vicar General's Papers, vol. I.

MIDDLESEX GUILDHALL:

Sessions Rolls, 355/38; 630/61, 194, 235, 252; 631/103; 636/88.
Sessions Register, IV. 206, 214.
Gaol Delivery Register, vol. 3, fols. 128b, 129b, 131, 133b, 136b, 137.
Gaol Delivery Roll, 636/92.

SOCIETY OF ANTIQUARIES:

Broadsides, James I–Charles I; vol. 21, No. 243.

BRITISH MUSEUM:

Add. MS. 19356.

NORTHAMPTON PROBATE REGISTRY:

Book A–V. 1621–8, p. 309.

GUILSBOROUGH, NORTHAMPTONSHIRE:

Parish Register.

Chap. III. (ii) *Michael and Frances* in Yorkshire

PUBLIC RECORD OFFICE:

Star Chamber; *Proceedings,* * 5. S. 30/16; * 8. 276/26.
Chancery; C. 142. 353/64.

(iii) *Fool's Fortune* in Shropshire

PUBLIC RECORD OFFICE:

Star Chamber; *Proceedings,* * 8. 250/31.

Chap. IV. (ii) *The Wells May Game*

PUBLIC RECORD OFFICE:

Star Chamber; *Proceedings,* * 8. 161/1 (Parts 1–7).

HUNTINGTON LIBRARY:

Ellesmere MS. 44, No. 2728.

Chap. V.   (ii) *The Old Guard at Stratford*

PUBLIC RECORD OFFICE:

Star Chamber; *Proceedings*, * 8. 26/10.

(iii) *Hudibras in Nottingham*

PUBLIC RECORD OFFICE:

Star Chamber; *Proceedings*, * 8. 27/7.

II. *NOTES UPON THE TUNES*

Chap. II.   (ii) *The Blazing Torch.*

I find no record elsewhere of this tune.

Chap. III.   (ii) *Michael and Frances.*

(a) *Phillida Flouts Me.*

This well-known tune is described in 1612 as a 'new tune', in *The Crown Garland of Golden Roses*, in which a 'sonnet' upon the death of Queen Elizabeth is set to it. The tune, and the original ballad sung to it, had however reached Yorkshire before 1602, and must have had a considerable vogue before that date to be used in this provincial jig. The ballad is printed in the *Roxburgh Ballads* (VI. 460–3). The Shirburn Castle MS. copy from which it is printed in Clarke's *Shirburn Ballads* (pp. 296–301) is dateable before 1615. The words and music are printed in Watts' *Musical Miscellany* (1729, II. 132).

The metre and rhyme scheme of the Yorkshire jig correspond exactly to that of the original, including the triple rhyme at the end of each stanza.

(b) *Fortune.*

This is clearly the famous tune to which *Fortune my Foe* was sung, and which is so often referred to in Elizabethan literature. Shakespeare mentions it in *The Merry Wives of Windsor*, in *Henry V*, and in *Twelfth Night*. Rowley, in *The Noble Soldier*, calls it 'the hanging tune', for many a criminal at the gallows composed his final lament (or the balladists for him) in this metre, and set his swan-song to this tune, for which it was eminently suitable.

The tune first appears in *Queen Elizabeth's Virginal Book*, and words and music are reprinted in the *Bagford Ballads*, from the Bagford MS. in the British Museum. The tune is the same as that referred to under the name of *Dr Faustus* and *Aim not too high*.

(c) *Take thy old Cloak about thee*.

This tune has been immortalized by Shakespeare in *Othello* (ii. 3), where it is sung by Iago to the words 'King Stephen was a worthy peer'. It is found in the Percy Folio MS., and is printed in Hales and Furnivall, *Percy Folio MS.* (ii. 320–4).

(d) *The Ladies of Essex Lamentation*.

It is possible that this is some hitherto unrecorded tune. But it is more likely to be a confusion between a tune *Essex's Last Good-night*, to which was set a lament upon the death of the Earl of Essex who died in 1576, and another, known as *Well-a-day*, to which was set, among others, 'A lamentable dittie composed upon the death of Lord Devereux, late Earl of Essex', after his execution in 1601. This suggestion is fortified by the occurrence of a song in *The Crown Garland* upon 'The dolefull death of Queen Jane, wife of Henry VIII', set to the tune of *The Lamentation of the Lord of Essex*. The substitution of *Ladies* for *Lord* is a very possible result of a generation or two of oral transmission.

The metre here falls into two groups, the first of nine lines, with some variation from the normal rhyming eights in the last three lines, and the second of eight regular eights. The rhymes, however, are in couplets, not alternate as in *Essex's Last Good-night*, which is obviously the tune intended here, and not *Well-a-day*, which is in sixes.

(e) *For her Apron*.

I find no record elsewhere of this tune.

(f) *The Cobbler*.

The metre here corresponds to none of the *Cobbler* tunes listed in Chappell's *Popular Music*. But the metrical scheme is actually that of *Phillida Flouts Me*, with its ending in a triple rhyme and short final line, though the final line has an added foot here.

Chap. III. (iii) *Fool's Fortune.*

(a) *A.B.C.*

The metre here is rhymed eights. We have on record *A godly and Christian A.B.C.*, set to the tune of *Rogero*, *The A.B.C. of a Priest*, and *The Aged Man's A.B.C.* *Rogero*, according to one extant example, was in rhymed eights and sixes. The *A.B.C.* was probably a variant of *Rogero*.

(b) *Barnaby.*

I find no record of the tune to which this doggerel verse was set.

(c) *Jockey there Man.*

The metre here resembles that of a song recorded as *Fife and a' the lands about it*, or alternatively under the titles of *Fairest Jenney* or *Jockey and Jenny*, as an Anglo-Scottish song. It was first printed in 1691, as an original composition, both with respect to words and music. But no conclusion can be drawn from this.

Chap. V. (iii) *Bonny Nell.*

This is evidently the well-known tune of *Bonny Nell*, the music of which may be found in Chappell's *Popular Music* (II. 502), set to words beginning 'as I went forth one summer's day'. The metre corresponds here, and the satire or song divides up into stanzas of six lines, as does *Bonny Nell*.

INDEX

(In a few cases indications of age have been supplied from sources not otherwise used here)

PRINTED BY
WALTER LEWIS, M.A.

AT THE
UNIVERSITY PRESS
CAMBRIDGE